Hong Kong Bankruptcy Ordinance

International Law & Taxation Publishers

London

Hong Kong Bankruptcy Ordinance

ISBN 1-893713-30-X

Copyright © 2001 International Law & Taxation Publishers

International Law & Taxation Publishers
London

http://www.internationallawandtaxationpublishers.com

Contents

BANKRUPTCY ORDINANCE

CHAPTER 6

ARRANGEMENT OF SECTIONS

Part I - Short Title And Interpretation

Part II - Proceedings From Act Of Bankruptcy To Discharge

Acts of bankruptcy

Receiving order and Official Receiver

Proceedings consequent on order

Public examination of debtor

Compositions and schemes of arrangement

Adjudication of bankruptcy

Control over person and property of debtor

Part III - Administration Of Property

Proof of debts

Property available for payment of debts

Part VII - Supplemental Provisions

Disobedience to order of court

Application of Ordinance

General rules

Fees and remuneration

Evidence

Miscellaneous

To amend the law relating to bankruptcy.

Note: The references to "Form 2", etc. are to the forms specified in the Bankruptcy

(Forms) Rules (Cap. 6 sub. leg.).

PART I - Short Title And Interpretation

Short title

1.   This Ordinance may be cited as the Bankruptcy Ordinance.

Interpretation

2.   In this Ordinance, unless the context otherwise requires-

"affidavit" includes statutory declaration, affirmation and attestation on honour;

"available act of bankruptcy" means any act of bankruptcy available for a bankruptcy petition at the date of the presentation of the petition on which the receiving order is made;

"bailiff" includes any officer charged with the execution of a writ or other process;

"court" means the High Court sitting in its bankruptcy jurisdiction;

"debt provable in bankruptcy" or "provable debt" includes any debt or liability by this Ordinance made provable in bankruptcy;

"goods" includes all chattels personal;

"oath" includes affirmation, declaration and attestation on honour;

"Official Receiver" means the Official Receiver appointed under section 75;

"ordinary resolution" means a resolution decided by a majority in value of the creditors present, personally or by proxy, at a meeting of creditors and voting on the resolution;

"prescribed" means prescribed by general rules within the meaning of this Ordinance;

"property" includes money, goods, things in action, land and every description of operty, whether real or personal and whether situate in Hong Kong or elsewhere, also obligations, easements and every description of estate, interest and profit, present or future, vested or contingent, arising out of or incident to property as above defined;

"Registrar" means the Registrar of the Supreme Court, and any Deputy or Assistant Registrar of the Supreme Court;

"resolution" means ordinary resolution;

"secured creditor" means a person holding a mortgage, charge or lien on the property of the debtor or any part thereof, as a security for a debt due to him from the debtor;

"special resolution" means a resolution decided by a majority in number and three-fourths in value of the creditors present, personally or by proxy, at a meeting of creditors and voting on the resolution;

"trustee" means the trustee in bankruptcy of a debtor's estate.

PART II - Proceedings From Act Of Bankruptcy To Discharge

Acts of bankruptcy

3.(1)　A debtor commits an act of bankruptcy in each of the following cases-

(a)　if in Hong Kong or elsewhere he makes a conveyance or assignment of his property to a trustee or trustees for the benefit of his creditors generally;

(b)　if in Hong Kong or elsewhere he makes a fraudulent conveyance, gift, delivery or transfer of his property or of any part thereof;

(c)　if in Hong Kong or elsewhere he makes any conveyance or transfer of his property or any part thereof, or creates any charge thereon, which would be void as a fraudulent preference if he were adjudged bankrupt;

(d)　if with intent to defeat or delay his creditors he does any of the following things, namely, departs out of Hong Kong, or being out of Hong Kong remains out of Hong Kong, or departs from his dwelling-house or usual place of business, or otherwise absents himself, or begins to keep house, or removes his property or any part thereof beyond the jurisdiction of the court;

(e)　if execution against him has been levied by seizure of his goods under process in an action, or proceeding in the court, and the goods have been either sold or held by the bailiff for 21 days:

Provided that, where an interpleader summons has been taken out in regard to the goods seized, the time elapsing between the date at which such summons is taken out and the date at which the proceedings on such summons are finally disposed of, settled or abandoned shall not be taken into account in calculating such period of 21 days;

(f)　if he files in the court a declaration of his inability to pay his debts or presents a bankruptcy petition against himself; (*See*

Form 2)

(g)　if a creditor has obtained a final judgment or final order against him for any amount, and execution thereon not having been stayed, has served on him in Hong Kong or, by leave of the

11

court, elsewhere, a bankruptcy notice under this Ordinance, and he does not, within 7 days after service of the notice, in case the service is effected in Hong Kong, and in case the service is effected elsewhere, then within the time limited in that behalf by the order giving leave to effect the service, either comply with the requirements of the notice or satisfy the court that he has a counter-claim set off or cross demand which equals or exceeds the amount of the judgment debt or sum ordered to be paid, and which he could not set up in the action in which the judgment was obtained or the proceedings in which the order was obtained:

For the purposes of this paragraph and of section 4, any person who is for the time being entitled to enforce a final judgement or final order shall be deemed to be a creditor who has obtained a final judgment or final order;

(h)   if the debtor gives notice to any of his creditors that he has suspended or that he is about to suspend payment of his debts.

(2) In this Ordinance, "a debtor", unless the context otherwise requires, includes any person, whether a British subject or not, who at the time when any act of bankruptcy was done or suffered by him-

(a)   was personally present in Hong Kong; or

(b)   ordinarily resided or had a place of residence in Hong Kong; or

(c)   was carrying on business in Hong Kong, personally or by means of an agent or manager; or

(d)   was a member of a firm or partnership which carried on business in Hong Kong.

Bankruptcy notices

4. A bankruptcy notice under this Ordinance shall be issued to a judgement creditor, or creditor who has obtained a final order, by the Registrar on the filing of a request for that purpose, and shall be in the prescribed form, and shall require the debtor to pay the judgment debt or sum ordered to be paid in accordance with the terms of the judgment or order, or to secure or compound for it to the satisfaction of the creditor or the court, and shall state the consequences of non-compliance with the notice, and shall be served in the prescribed manner: (*See Forms 4, 5*)

Provided that a bankruptcy notice-

(a)   may specify an agent to act on behalf of the creditor in respect

of any payment or other thing required by the notice to be made to, or done to the satisfaction of, the creditor;

(b)   shall not be invalidated by reason only that the sum specified in the notice as the amount due exceeds the amount actually due, unless the debtor within the time allowed for payment gives notice to the creditor that he disputes the validity of the notice on the ground of such misstatement; but if the debtor does not give such notice, he shall be deemed to have complied with the bankruptcy notice if within the time allowed he takes such steps as would have constituted a compliance with the notice had the actual amount due been correctly specified therein.

Receiving order and Official Receiver

Jurisdiction to make receiving order

5. Subject to the conditions hereinafter specified, if a debtor commits an act of bankruptcy the court may, on a bankruptcy petition being presented either by a creditor or by the debtor, make an order, in this Ordinance called a receiving order, for the protection of the estate. (*See Forms 25, 26*)

Conditions on which creditor may petition

6.(1) Subject to the provisions of section 7, a creditor shall not be entitled to present a bankruptcy petition against a debtor unless- (*See Form 10*)

(a)   the debt owing by the debtor to the petitioning creditor, or if 2 or more creditors join in the petition, the aggregate amount of debts owing to the several petitioning creditors, amounts to more than $5,000; and

(b)   the debt is a liquidated sum, payable either immediately or at some certain future time; and

(c)   the act of bankruptcy on which the petition is grounded has occurred within 3 months before the presentation of the petition; and

(d)   the debtor is domiciled in Hong Kong, or within a year before the date of the presentation of the petition has ordinarily resided, or had a dwelling-house or place of business, in Hong Kong, or has carried on business in Hong Kong, personally or by means of an agent or manager, or is or within the said period has been a member of a firm or partnership of persons which has carried on business in Hong Kong by means of a partner or partners or an agent or manager.

(2) If the petitioning creditor is a secured creditor, he must in his petition either state that he is willing to give up his security for the benefit of the creditors in the event of the debtor being adjudged bankrupt, or give an estimate of the value of his security. In the latter case he may be admitted as a petitioning creditor to the extent of the balance of the debt due to him after deducting the value so estimated in the same manner as if he were an unsecured creditor.

Liability of firm to have receiving order made against it

7.(1) The following provisions shall have effect in the case of a firm carrying on business in Hong Kong-

(a) a creditor of the firm shall be entitled to present a bankruptcy petition against the firm, and a receiving order may be made against the firm in respect of an act of bankruptcy committed in reference to the business of the firm by any partner of the firm or by any person having the control or management of the business of the firm. An act of bankruptcy shall be deemed to be committed in reference to the business of the firm in all cases in which the act relates to the property or creditors of the firm and would be an act of bankruptcy by such partner or person as aforesaid if it related to his property or creditors;

(b) it shall be sufficient that a receiving order against the firm be made in the firm name, without mentioning the names of the partners, and such receiving order shall affect the joint and separate property of all the partners;

(c) the right of a creditor to present a bankruptcy petition against the firm, and the jurisdiction of the court to make a receiving order or an adjudication of bankruptcy against the firm, shall not be affected by the fact, if it is so, that all or any of the partners of the firm are not British subjects or are not resident or domiciled in Hong Kong.

(2) The provisions of this section shall, so far as the nature of the case will permit, apply to any person carrying on business in Hong Kong in a name or style other than his own name.

Powers of Official Receiver and duties

of debtor on petition being filed

8.(1) Immediately on the filing of any petition the Official Receiver may, in cases where he has reason to believe that any offence under this Ordinance or any fraud has been or is about to be perpetrated, by notice sent by messenger or by ordinary post, summon the debtor to attend before him to give such information as he requires, and may, either by himself or his agent authorized by him in writing, enter on any premises occupied by the debtor between the hours of 8 a.m. and 6 p.m. for the purpose of inspecting his property, stock in trade and books of account.

(2) It shall be the duty of the debtor to furnish the Official Receiver with all such information as it is in the debtor's power to give or to obtain.

(3) If the debtor fails without reasonable cause to attend on the OfficialReceiver as aforesaid or to furnish him with such information as aforesaid, or if the debtor obstructs the search of the premises or the production of any book or document required in connexion therewith, or authorizes or permits any such obstruction, the debtor shall be liable on summary conviction to imprisonment for any term not exceeding 6 months, and every person who takes any part in any such obstruction, whether authorized or permitted by the debtor or not, shall be liable to the like penalty.

Creditor's petition and order thereon

9.(1) A creditor's petition shall be verified by affidavit of the creditor or of some person on his behalf having knowledge of the facts, and shall be served in the prescribed manner. (*See Forms 10, 10A, 11, 12*)

(2) At the hearing the court shall require proof of the debt of the petitioning creditor, of the service of the petition and of the act of bankruptcy, or if more than one act of bankruptcy is alleged in the petition, of some one of the alleged acts of bankruptcy, and if satisfied with the proof, may make a receiving order in pursuance of the petition.

(3) If the court is not satisfied with the proof of the petitioning creditor's debt or of the act of bankruptcy or of the service of the petition, or is satisfied by the debtor that he is able to pay his debts, or considers that for other sufficient cause no order ought to be made, the court may dismiss the petition.

(4) When the act of bankruptcy relied on is non-compliance with a bankruptcy notice to pay, secure or compound for a judgment debt or sum ordered to be paid, the court may, if it thinks fit, stay or dismiss the petition on the ground that an appeal is pending from the judgment or order.

(5) Where the debtor appears on the petition and denies that he is indebted to the petitioner, or that he is indebted to such an amount as would justify the petitioner in presenting a petition against him, the court, on such security (if any) being given as the court may require for payment to the petitioner of any debt which may be established against him in due course of law, and of the costs of establishing the debt, may, instead of dismissing the petition, stay all proceedings on the petition for such time as may be required for trial of the question relating to the debt.

(6) Where proceedings are stayed the court may, if by reason of the delay caused by the stay of proceedings or for any other cause it thinks just, make a receiving order on the petition of some other creditor, and shall thereupon dismiss, on such terms as it thinks just, the petition in which proceedings have been stayed as aforesaid.

(7) A creditor's petition shall not after presentment be withdrawn without the leave of the court.

Debtor's petition and order thereon

10.(1) A debtor's petition shall allege that the debtor is unable to pay his debts, and the presentation thereof shall be deemed an act of bankruptcy without the previous filing by the debtor of any declaration of inability to pay his debts, and the court shall thereupon make a receiving order: (*See Form 3*)

Provided that the court in its discretion may refuse the order if it considers that there is sufficient cause for no order to be made.

In this subsection "sufficient cause" shall be deemed to include, *inter alia*, the non-attendance of the debtor, or in the case of a firm, of at least one of the partners thereof, on the hearing of the petition, the absence of any material book of account, or any fraud or misconduct not amounting to fraud by the debtor in relation to his affairs, or in the case of a firm or person carrying on business under a Chinese firm name, the non-production of the partnership book or of the receipt and money-payment chops used in connexion with the business.

(2) A debtor's petition shall not after presentment be withdrawn withoutthe leave of the court.

Appearance of Official Receiver on petition

11. On the hearing of any creditor's or debtor's petition it shall be lawful for the Official Receiver to appear and to call, examine and cross-examine any witness and, if he so thinks fit, to support or oppose the making of a receiving order.

Effect of receiving order

12.(1) On the making of a receiving order the Official Receiver shall be thereby constituted receiver of the property of the debtor, and thereafter, except as directed by this Ordinance, no creditor to whom the debtor is indebted in respect of any debt provable in bankruptcy shall have any remedy against the property or person of the debtor in respect of the debt, or shall commence any action or other legal proceedings, unless with the leave of the court and on such terms as the court may impose.

(2) This section shall not affect the power of any secured creditor to realize or otherwise deal with his security.

Power to appoint interim receiver

13. The court may, if it is shown to be necessary for the protection of the estate, at any time after the presentation of a bankruptcy petition and before a receiving order is made, appoint the Official Receiver to be interim receiver of the property of the debtor or of any part thereof, and direct him to take immediate possession thereof or of any part thereof. (*See Form 13*)

Power to stay pending proceedings

14.(1) The court may at any time after the presentation of a bankruptcy petition either stay any action, execution or other legal process against the property or person of the debtor or allow it to continue on such terms as it may think just.

(2) Where the court makes an order staying any action or proceedings or staying proceedings generally, the order may be served by sending a copy thereof, under the seal of the court, by post to the address for service of the plaintiff or other party prosecuting such proceeding or to the address of his solicitor.

(3) Without prejudice to the provisions of subsection (1), if the court orders the release of any debtor who is under execution for a civil debt, it may impose such conditions as it thinks fit, and in particular it may require as a condition of such release that the debtor find security to attend in the subsequent bankruptcy proceedings and to abide by all orders of the court relating to the said proceedings.

Power to appoint special manager

15.(1) The court may, on the application of the Official Receiver or of any creditor or creditors, and if satisfied that the nature of the debtor's estate or business or the interests of the creditors generally require the appointment of a special manager of the estate or business other than the Official Receiver, appoint a manager thereof accordingly to act until a trustee is appointed, and with such powers (including any of the powers of a receiver) as may be entrusted to him by the Official Receiver.

(2) The special manager shall give security and account in such manner as the court may direct.

(3) The special manager shall receive such remuneration as may be prescribed.

Advertisement of receiving order

16. Notice of every receiving order, stating the name, address and description of the debtor, the date of the order, and the date of the petition, shall be gazetted by the Official Receiver. (*See Form 27*)

Proceedings consequent on order
First and other meetings of creditors

17.(1) As soon as may be after the making of a receiving order against a debtor a general meeting of his creditors (in this Ordinance referred to as the first meeting of creditors) shall be held for the purpose of considering whether a proposal for a composition or scheme of arrangement shall be accepted, or whether it is expedient that the debtor shall be adjudged bankrupt, and generally as to the mode of dealing with the debtor's property. (*See Forms 30, 31, 32, 39, 45*)

(2) The Chief Justice may, with the approval of Legislative Council, make rules providing for the summoning of and proceedings at the first and other meetings of creditors.

Debtor's statement of affairs

18.(1) Where a receiving order is made against a debtor, he shall, unless the court otherwise orders, make out and submit to the Official Receiver a statement of and in relation to his affairs in the prescribed form, verified by affidavit, and showing the particulars of the debtor's assets, debts and liabilities, wherever situate, the names, addresses and occupations of his creditors, whether in Hong Kong or elsewhere, the securities held by them respectively, the dates when the securities were respectively given, and such further or other information as may be prescribed or as the Official Receiver may require. Such statement shall also give details of all property held by him in a t'ong name or under any alias, or by his wife or any concubine of his, or by any person in trust for him or them, with full particulars as to the manner and date of its being acquired. (*See Form 28*)

(2) The statement shall be so submitted within the following times, namely-

        (a)   if the order is made on the petition of the debtor, within 3 days from the date of the order;

        (b)   if the order is made on the petition of a creditor, within 7 days from the date of the order,

but the court may, in either case for special reasons, extend the time.

(3) If the debtor fails without reasonable excuse to comply with the requirements of this section, he may be punished for a contempt of court and the court may, on the application of the Official Receiver or of any creditor, adjudge him bankrupt. (*See Form 75*)

(4) Any person stating himself to be a creditor of the bankrupt may, on payment of the prescribed fee, personally or by agent inspect the statement at all reasonable times and take any copy thereof or extract therefrom, but any person untruthfully so stating himself to be a creditor shall be guilty of a contempt of court and shall be punishable accordingly on the application of the trustee or Official Receiver.

Public examination of debtor

19.(1) Where the court makes a receiving order, it shall, save as in this Ordinance provided, hold a public sitting, on a day to be appointed by the court, for the examination of the debtor, and the debtor shall attend thereat and shall be examined as to his conduct, dealings and property. (*See Forms 52 to 63*)

(2) The examination shall be held as soon as conveniently may be after the expiration of the time for the submission of the debtor's statement of affairs.

(3) The court may adjourn the examination from time to time.

(4) Any creditor who has tendered a proof, or his representative authorized in writing, may question the debtor concerning his affairs and the causes of his failure.

(5) The Official Receiver shall take part in the examination of the debtor, and for the purpose thereof, if specially authorized by the court, may employ a solicitor with or without counsel. No solicitor or counsel shall be allowed to take part in the examination on behalf of the debtor.

(6) If a trustee is appointed before the conclusion of the examination, hemay take part therein.

(7) The court may put such questions to the debtor as it may think expedient.

(8) The debtor shall be examined upon oath and it shall be his duty to answer all such questions as the court may put or allow to be put to him. Such notes of the examination as the court thinks proper shall be taken down either in shorthand or longhand and they or a transcript thereof shall be read over either to or by the debtor and signed by him and may thereafter, save as in this Ordinance provided, be used in evidence against him; they shall also be open to the inspection of any creditor at all reasonable times upon payment of the prescribed fee.

(9) When the court is of opinion that the affairs of the debtor have been sufficiently investigated, it shall by order declare that his examination is concluded, but such order shall not be made until after the day appointed for the first meeting of creditors.

(10) Where the debtor is a lunatic or suffers from any such mental or physical affliction or disability as in the opinion of the court makes him unfit to attend his public examination, or is absent from Hong Kong, the court may make an order dispensing with such examination or directing that the debtor be examined on such, terms, in such manner and at such place as to the court seems expedient.

Power of court to dispense with public examination
of debtor on application of Official Receiver

19A.(1) Notwithstanding section 19 the court may, on the application of theOfficial Receiver, make an order dispensing with the public examination of the debtor.

(2) Before making an application under subsection (1) the Official Receiver shall-

        (a)   publish notice of his intention to make the application in the Gazette; and

        (b)   give notice of his intention to make the application to every creditor who has tendered a proof.

(3) Any creditor who has tendered a proof and wishes to oppose the making of an order under subsection (1) shall, within 21 days after the date of publication of a notice pursuant to subsection (2), give notice in writing to the Official Receiver of his intention to oppose the making of an order and may thereafter appear and oppose the making of an order.

(4) Before making an order under subsection (1) the court shall consider a report of the Official Receiver made in the manner prescribed.

Composition and schemes of arrangement
Compositions and schemes of arrangement

20.(1) Where a debtor intends to make a proposal for a composition in satisfaction of his debts or a proposal for a scheme of arrangement of his affairs, he shall, within 4 days of submitting his statement of affairs or within such time thereafter as the Official Receiver may fix, lodge with the Official Receiver a proposal in writing, signed by him, embodying the terms of the composition or scheme which he is desirous of submitting for the consideration of his creditors and setting out particulars of any sureties or securities proposed.

(2) In such case the Official Receiver shall hold a meeting of creditors before the public examination of the debtor is concluded, and send to each creditor before the meeting a copy of the debtor's proposal with a report thereon; and if at that meeting a majority in number and three-fourths in value of all the creditors who have proved resolve to accept the proposal, it shall be deemed to be duly accepted by the creditors, and when approved by the court shall be binding on all the creditors. (*See Forms 64, 65, 66*)

(3) The debtor may at the meeting amend the terms of his proposal, if the amendment is in the opinion of the Official Receiver calculated to benefit the general body of creditors.

(4) Any creditor who has proved his debt may assent to or dissent from the proposal by a letter addressed to the Official Receiver so as to be received by him not later than the day preceding the meeting, and any such assent or dissent shall have effect as if the creditor had been present and had voted at the meeting.

(5) The debtor or the Official Receiver may, after the proposal is accepted by the creditors, apply to the court to approve it, and notice of the time appointed for hearing the application shall be given to each creditor who has proved. (*See Form 68*)

(6) The application shall not be heard until after the public examination of the debtor has been concluded, or dispensed with under section 19A. Any creditor who has proved may be heard by the court in opposition to the application, notwithstanding that he may at a meeting of creditors have voted for the acceptance of the proposal.

(7) For the purpose of approving a composition or scheme by joint debtors the court may, if it thinks fit and on the report of the Official Receiver that it is expedient so to do, dispense with the public examination of any of the joint debtors if they are or any one of them is prevented from attending the examination by illness or absence from Hong Kong but one at least of such joint debtors shall be publicly examined.

(8) The court shall before approving the proposal hear a report of the Official Receiver as to the terms thereof and as to the conduct of the debtor, and any objections which may be made by or on behalf of any creditor.

(9) If the court is of opinion that the terms of the proposal are not reasonable or are not calculated to benefit the general body of creditors, the court shall refuse to approve the proposal.

(10) If any facts are proved on proof of which the court would be requiredeither to refuse, suspend or attach conditions to the debtor's discharge were headjudged bankrupt, the court shall refuse to approve the proposal unless itprovides reasonable security for the payment of not less than 25 per cent on all the unsecured debts provable against the debtor's estate.

(11) In any other case the court may either approve or refuse to approve the proposal.

(12) If the court approves the proposal, the approval may be testified by the seal of the court being attached to the instrument containing the terms of the proposed composition or scheme, or by the terms being embodied in an order of the court.

(See Form 70)

(13) A composition or scheme accepted and approved in pursuance of this section shall be binding on all the creditors so far as relates to any debts due to them from the debtor and provable in bankruptcy.

(14) A certificate of the Official Receiver that a composition or scheme has been duly accepted and approved shall, in the absence of fraud, be conclusive as to its validity.

(15) The provisions of a composition or scheme under this section may be enforced by the court on application by any person interested, and any disobedience of an order of the court made on the application shall be deemed a contempt of court. *(See Forms 72, 73, 98, 101)*

(16) If default is made in payment of any instalment due in pursuance of the composition or scheme, or if it appears to the court on satisfactory evidence that the composition or scheme cannot, in consequence of legal difficulties or for any sufficient cause, proceed without injustice or undue delay to the creditors or to the debtor, or that the approval of the court was obtained by fraud, the court may, if it thinks fit, on application by the Official Receiver or the trustee or by any creditor, adjudge the debtor bankrupt and annul the composition or scheme, but without prejudice to the validity of any sale, disposition or payment duly made or thing duly done under or in pursuance of the composition or scheme. Where a debtor is adjudged bankrupt under this subsection, any debt provable in other respects, which has been contracted before the adjudication, shall be provable in the bankruptcy.

(17) If under or in pursuance of a composition or scheme a trustee is appointed to administer the debtor's property or manage his business or to distribute the composition, section 29 and Part V shall apply as if the trustee were a trustee in a bankruptcy and as if the terms "bankruptcy", "bankrupt" and "order of adjudication" included respectively a composition or scheme of arrangement, a compounding or arranging debtor and an order approving the composition or scheme.

(18) Part III shall, so far as the nature of the case and the terms of the composition or scheme admit, apply thereto, the same interpretation being given to the words "trustee", "bankruptcy", "bankrupt" and "order of adjudication", as in subsection (17).

(19) No composition or scheme shall be approved by the court which does not provide for the payment in priority to other debts of all debts directed to be so paid in the distribution of the property of a bankrupt.

(20) The acceptance by a creditor of a composition or scheme shall not release any person who under this Ordinance would not be released by an order of discharge if the debtor had been adjudged bankrupt.

Effect of composition or scheme

21. Notwithstanding the acceptance and approval of a composition or scheme, the composition or scheme shall not be binding on any creditor so far as regards a debt or liability from which under the provisions of this Ordinance the debtor would not be released by an order of discharge in bankruptcy, unless the creditor assents to the composition or scheme.

Adjudication of bankruptcy
Adjudication of bankruptcy where composition
not accepted or not approved

22.(1) Where a receiving order is made against a debtor, then if the creditors at the first meeting or any adjournment thereof by ordinary resolution resolve that the debtor be adjudged bankrupt, or pass no resolution, or if the creditors do not meet, or if a composition or scheme is not approved in pursuance of this Ordinance within 14 days after the conclusion of the examination of the debtor or such further time as the court may allow, the court shall adjudge the debtor bankrupt; and thereupon the property of the bankrupt shall become divisible among his creditors and shall vest in a trustee.

(2) Notice of every order adjudging a debtor bankrupt, stating the name, address and description of the bankrupt, the date of the adjudication and the name of the trustee, shall be gazetted and shall be advertised in at least 2 local newspapers, one of which shall be Chinese, or as may be prescribed, and the date of the order shall for the purposes of this Ordinance be the date of the adjudication. (*See Form 27*)

(3) It shall be sufficient that an adjudication order against a firm be made in the firm name without mentioning the names of the partners, and such adjudication order shall affect the joint and separate property of all the partners. (*See Form 78*)

Appointment of trustee

23.(1) Where a debtor is adjudged bankrupt or the creditors have resolved that he be adjudged bankrupt, the creditors may by ordinary resolution appoint the Official Receiver or some other fit person, whether a creditor or not, to fill the office of trustee of the property of the bankrupt or they may resolve to leave his appointment to the committee of inspection hereinafter mentioned. A person shall be deemed not fit to act as trustee of the property of a bankrupt where he has been previously removed from the office of trustee of a bankrupt's property for misconduct or neglect of duty.

(2) The person appointed shall, unless he is the Official Receiver, give such security as the court may direct or as may be prescribed, and the court, if satisfied with the security, shall certify under the hand of the Registrar that his appointment has been duly made, unless the appointment is disapproved by the court on the ground that it has not been made in good faith by a majority in value of the creditors voting, or that the person appointed is not fit to act as trustee, or that his connexion with or relation to the bankrupt or his estate or any particular creditor makes it difficult for him to act with impartiality in the interests of the creditors generally.

(3) The appointment of a trustee shall take effect as from the date of the certificate.

(4) When a debtor is adjudged bankrupt after the first meeting of creditors has been held and a trustee has not been appointed prior to the adjudication, the Official Receiver shall forthwith summon a meeting of creditors for the purpose of appointing a trustee. If no trustee is then appointed by the creditors the court shall on the application of the Official Receiver appoint the Official Receiver or some other fit person to be trustee.

Committee of inspection

24.(1) The creditors qualified to vote may at their first or any subsequent meeting, by resolution, appoint a committee of inspection for the purpose of superintending the administration of the bankrupt's property by the trustee.

(2) The committee of inspection shall consist of 2 or more persons, possessing one or other of the following qualifications-

(a)   that of being a creditor or the holder of a general proxy or general power of attorney from a creditor:

> Provided that no creditor and no holder of a general proxy or general power of attorney from a creditor shall be qualified to act as a member of the committee of inspection until the creditor has proved his debt and the proof has been admitted; or

(b)   that of being a person to whom a creditor intends to give a general proxy or general power of attorney:

> Provided that no such person shall be qualified to act as a member of the committee of inspection until he holds such a proxy or power of attorney, and until the creditor has proved his debt and the proof has been admitted.

(3) The committee of inspection shall meet at such times as they shall from time to time appoint, and failing such appointment, at least once a month, and the trustee or any member of the committee may also call a meeting of the committee as and when he thinks necessary.

(4) The committee may act by a majority of their members present at a meeting, but shall not act unless a majority of the committee are present at the meeting.

(5) Any member of the committee may resign his office by notice in writing signed by him and delivered to the trustee.

(6) If a member of the committee becomes bankrupt, or compounds or arranges with his creditors, or is absent from 5 consecutive meetings of the committee, his office shall thereupon become vacant.

(7) Any member of the committee may be removed by an ordinary resolution at any meeting of creditors of which 7 days' notice has been given stating the object of the meeting.

(8) On a vacancy occurring in the office of a member of the committee the trustee shall forthwith summon a meeting of creditors for the purpose of filling the vacancy, and the meeting may by resolution appoint another creditor or other person eligible as above to fill the vacancy:

> Provided that if the trustee is of the opinion that it is unnecessary for the vacancy to be filled he may apply to the court and the court may make an order that the vacancy shall not be filled, or shall not be filled except in such circumstances as may be specified in the order.

(9) The continuing members of the committee, provided there be not less than 2 such continuing members, may act notwithstanding any vacancy in their body.

(10)   If there be no committee of inspection any act or thing or any direction or permission by this

Ordinance authorized or required to be done or given by the committee may be done or given by the court on the application of the trustee.

Power to accept composition or scheme after adjudication

25.(1) Where a debtor is adjudged bankrupt the creditors may, if they think fit, at any time after the adjudication, by a majority in number and three-fourths in value of all the creditors who have proved, resolve to accept a proposal for a composition in satisfaction of the debts due to them under the bankruptcy or for a scheme of arrangement of the bankrupt's affairs, and thereupon the same proceedings shall be taken and the same consequences shall ensue as in the case of a composition or scheme accepted before adjudication. (*See Forms 31, 64, 65, 66*)

(2) If the court approves the composition or scheme it may make an order annulling the bankruptcy and vesting the property of the bankrupt in him or in such other person as the court may appoint, on such terms and subject to such conditions, if any, as the court may declare.

(3) If default is made in payment of any instalment due in pursuance of the composition or scheme, or if it appears to the court that the composition or scheme cannot proceed without injustice or undue delay, or that the approval of the court was obtained by fraud, the court may, if it thinks fit, on application by any person interested, adjudge the debtor bankrupt and annul the composition or scheme, but without prejudice to the validity of any sale, disposition or payment duly made or thing duly done under or in pursuance of the composition or scheme. Where a debtor is adjudged bankrupt under this subsection, all debts, provable in other respects, which have been contracted before the date of such adjudication shall be provable in the bankruptcy.

Control over person and property of debtor

Duties of debtor as to discovery and realization of property

26.(1) Every debtor against whom a receiving order is made shall, unless prevented by sickness or other sufficient cause, attend the first meeting of his creditors, and shall submit to such examination and give such information as the meeting may require.

(2) He shall give such inventory of his property, such list of his creditors and debtors, and of the debts due to and from them respectively, submit to such examination in respect of his property or his creditors, attend such other meetings of his creditors, wait at such times on the Official Receiver, special manager or trustee, execute such powers of attorney, conveyances, deeds and instruments, and generally do all such acts and things in relation to his property and the distribution of the proceeds amongst his creditors, as may be reasonably required by the Official Receiver, special manager or trustee or may be provided by this Ordinance, or be prescribed or be directed by the court by any special order or orders made in reference to any particular case or made on the occasion of any special application by the Official Receiver, special manager, trustee or any creditor or person interested.

(3) He shall, if adjudged bankrupt, aid to the utmost of his power in the realization of his property and the distribution of the proceeds among his creditors.

(4) If a debtor wilfully fails to perform the duties imposed on him by this section or to deliver up possession of any part of his property, which is divisible amongst his creditors under this Ordinance and which is for the time being in his possession or under his control, to the Official Receiver or to the trustee or to any person authorized by the court to take possession of it, he shall, in addition to any other punishment to which he may be subject, be guilty of a contempt of court and may be punished accordingly. (*See Forms 99, 102, 104*)

Arrest of debtor under certain circumstances

27.(1) The court may, by warrant addressed to any person or persons named therein, cause a debtor to be arrested, and any books, papers, money and goods in his possession or under his control or relating to his affairs to be seized, and him and them to be safely kept as prescribed until such time as the court may order under the following circumstances- (*See Forms 109, 110*)

(a) if, after a bankruptcy notice has been issued under this Ordinance or after presentation of a bankruptcy petition by or against him, it appears to the court that there is probable cause for believing that he has absconded, or is about to abscond, with a view of avoiding payment of the debt in respect of which the bankruptcy notice was issued, or of avoiding service of a bankruptcy petition, or of avoiding appearance to any such petition, or of avoiding examination in respect of his affairs, or of otherwise avoiding, delaying or embarrassing proceedings in bankruptcy against him;

(b) if, after presentation of a bankruptcy petition by or against him, it appears to the court that there is probable cause for believing that he is about to dispose of or remove his goods with a view

to preventing or delaying possession being taken of them by the Official Receiver or trustee, or that there is probable ground for believing that he has concealed or is about to conceal or destroy any of his goods or any books, documents or writings which might be of use to his creditors in the course of his bankruptcy;

(c) if, after service of a bankruptcy petition on him or after a receiving order is made against him he removes any goods in his possession above the value of $50 without the leave of the Official Receiver or trustee;

(d) if without good cause shown he fails to attend any examination ordered by the court;

(e)   if there is probable cause for believing that he has committed an offence punishable under this Ordinance:

Provided that no arrest upon a bankruptcy notice shall be valid and protected unless the debtor before or at the time of his arrest is served with such bankruptcy notice.

(2)   No payment or composition made or security given after arrest made under this section shall be exempt from the provisions of this Ordinance relating to fraudulent preferences.

Re-direction of debtor's telegrams and letters

28.   Where a receiving order is made against a debtor the court, on theapplication of the Official Receiver or trustee, may from time to time order that for such time, not exceeding 3 months, as the court thinks fit telegrams and post letters and other postal packets, addressed to the debtor at any place or places mentioned in the order for re-direction, shall be re-directed, sent or delivered by the agent of the telegraph organization or the Post-master General, or the officers acting under them, to the Official Receiver or the trustee or otherwise as the court directs, and the same shall be done accordingly. (*See Form 111*)

Inquiry as to debtor's conduct, dealings and property

29.(1) The court may, on the application of the Official Receiver or trustee, at any time after a receiving order has been made against a debtor summon before it the debtor or his wife, or any person known or suspected to have in his possession any of the estate or effects belonging to the debtor or supposed to be indebted to the debtor, or any person whom the court may deem capable of giving information respecting the debtor, his dealings or property, and the court may require any such person to produce any documents in his custody or power relating to the debtor, his dealings or property. (*See Form 112*)

(2) If any person so summoned, after having been tendered a reasonable sum, refuses to come before the court at the time appointed, or refuses to produce any such document, having no lawful impediment made known to the court at the time of its sitting and allowed by it, the court may, by warrant, cause him to be apprehended and brought up for examination. (*See Forms 115, 116*)

(3) The court may, by itself or by a commissioner appointed for the purpose, examine on oath, either by word of mouth or by written interrogatories, any person so brought before it concerning the debtor, his dealings or property.

(4) If any person on examination before the court admits that he is indebted to the debtor, the court may, on the application of the Official Receiver or trustee, order him to pay to the Official Receiver or trustee, at such time and in such manner as to the court seems expedient, the amount admitted or any part thereof, either in full discharge of the whole amount in question or not, as the court thinks fit, with or without costs of the examination. (*See Forms 113,114*)

(5) If any person on examination before the court admits that he has in his possession any property

belonging to the debtor, the court may, on the application of the Official Receiver or trustee, order him to deliver to the Official Receiver or trustee such property or any part thereof, at such time and in such manner and on such terms as to the court may seem just.

(6) The court may, if it thinks fit, order that any person who if in Hong Kong would be liable to be brought before it under this section shall be examined in any place out of Hong Kong by a commissioner appointed for the purpose.

(7) In the case of the death of the debtor or his wife or of any other witness whose evidence has been duly taken under this Ordinance, the deposition of the person so deceased purporting to be sealed with the seal of the court, or a copy thereof purporting to be so sealed, shall in all legal proceedings be admitted as evidence of the matters therein deposed to, saving all just exceptions.

Discharge of bankrupt

30.(1) A bankrupt may, at any time after being adjudged bankrupt, apply to the court for an order of discharge, and the court shall appoint a day for hearing the application, but the application shall not be heard until the public examination of the bankrupt is concluded, or dispensed with under section 19A. The application shall, except when the court in accordance with rules under this Ordinance otherwise directs, be heard in open court.

(2) Where the bankrupt does not of his own accord, within such time as the court may deem reasonable, apply for his discharge, the court may, of its own motion or on the application of the Official Receiver or the trustee or any creditor who has proved, make an order calling upon the bankrupt to come up for his discharge on a day to be fixed by the court, and on due service of the order, if the bankrupt does not appear on the day fixed thereby, the court may make such order as it thinks fit, subject to the provisions of this section, and the debtor shall, in addition to any other punishment to which he may be subject, be guilty of a contempt of court and may be punished accordingly.

(3) On the hearing of the application, or on the day on which the bankrupt has been ordered to come up for his discharge or any subsequent day, the court shall take into consideration a report of the Official Receiver as to the bankrupt's conduct and affairs (including a report as to the bankrupt's conduct during the proceedings under his bankruptcy) and may either grant or refuse an absolute order of discharge, or suspend the operation of the order for a specified time, or grant an order of discharge subject to any conditions with respect to any earnings or income which may afterwards become due to the bankrupt or with respect to his after acquired property:

Provided that where the bankrupt has committed any indictable offence under this Ordinance or any other indictable offence connected with his bankruptcy, or where in any case any of the facts hereinafter mentioned are proved the court shall-

<blockquote>(a)   refuse the discharge; or</blockquote>

(b)   suspend the discharge for such period as the court thinks proper; or

(c)   suspend the discharge until a dividend of not less than 50 per cent has been paid to the creditors; or

(d)   require the bankrupt as a condition of his discharge to consent to judgment being entered against him by the Official Receiver or trustee for any balance or part of any balance of the debts provable under the bankruptcy which is not satisfied at the date of the discharge, such balance or part of any balance of the debts to be paid out of the future earnings or after acquired property of the bankrupt in such manner and subject to such conditions as the court may direct; but execution shall not be issued on the judgment without leave of the court, which leave may be given on proof that the bankrupt has since his discharge acquired property or income available towards payment of his debts:

Provided that, if at any time after the expiration of 2 years from the date of any order made under this section the bankrupt satisfies the court that there is no reasonable probability of his being in a position to comply with the terms of such order, the court may modify the terms of the order or of any substituted order in such manner and upon such conditions as it may think fit.

(4)   The facts hereinbefore referred to are-

(a)   that the bankrupt's assets are not of a value equal to 50 per cent of his unsecured liabilities, unless he satisfies the court that the fact that the assets are not of a value of 50 per cent of his unsecured liabilities has arisen from circumstances for which he cannot justly be held responsible;

(b)   that the bankrupt has omitted to keep such books of account as are usual and proper in the business carried on by him and as sufficiently disclose his business transactions and financial position within the 3 years immediately preceding his bankruptcy, or in the case of a firm carrying on business under a Chinese firm name, that a partnership book has not been kept, or that such books have not been available for the trustee during the bankruptcy proceedings, unless they have been accidentally lost or destroyed, the onus of proof of such accidental loss or destruction being on the bankrupt;

(c)   that the bankrupt has continued to trade after knowing himself to be insolvent;

(d)   that the bankrupt has contracted any debt provable in the bankruptcy without having at the time of contracting it any reasonable or probable ground of expectation (proof whereof shall lie on him) of being able to pay it;

(e)   that the bankrupt has failed to account satisfactorily for any loss of assets or for any deficiency of assets to meet his liabilities;

(f)   that the bankrupt has brought on or contributed to his bankruptcy by rash and hazardous speculations, or by unjustifiable extravagance in living, or by gambling, or by culpable neglect of his business affairs;

(g)   that the bankrupt has put any of his creditors to unnecessary expense by a frivolous or vexatious defence to any action properly brought against him;

(h)   that the bankrupt has brought on or contributed to his bankruptcy by incurring unjustifiable expense by bringing a frivolous or vexatious action;

(i)   that the bankrupt has within 3 months preceding the date of the receiving order, when unable to pay his debts as they become due, given an undue preference to any of his creditors;

(j)   that the bankrupt has within 3 months preceding the date of the receiving order incurred liabilities with a view to making his assets equal to 50 per cent of his unsecured liabilities;

(k)   that the bankrupt has on any previous occasion, whether in Hong Kong or elsewhere, been adjudged bankrupt or made a composition or arrangement with his creditors;

(l)   that the bankrupt has been guilty of any fraud or fraudulent breach of trust.

(5)   The court may, on proof to its satisfaction of any of the facts mentioned in subsection (4)(b), (c), (d), (f), (g), (h), (i) or (l), summarily sentence the bankrupt to imprisonment for 1 year.

(6)   For the purposes of this section, bankrupt's assets shall be deemed of a value equal to 50 per cent of his unsecured liabilities when the court is satisfied that the property of the bankrupt has realized or is likely to realize, or with due care in realization might have realized, an amount equal to 50 per cent of his unsecured liabilities, and a report by the Official Receiver or the trustee shall be prima facie evidence of the amount of such liabilities.

(7) For the purposes of this section, the report of the Official Receiver shall be prima facie evidence of the statements therein contained.

(8) Notice of the appointment by the court of the day for hearing the application for discharge shall be published as the court may direct or as may be prescribed and shall be sent 14 days at least before the day so appointed to each creditor who has proved, and the court may hear the Official Receiver and the trustee and may also hear any creditor. At the hearing the court may put such questions to the debtor and receive such evidence as it may think fit.

(9) The powers of suspending and of attaching conditions to a bankrupt's discharge may be exercised concurrently.

(10)   A discharged bankrupt shall, notwithstanding his discharge, give such assistance as the trustee may require in the realization and distribution of such of his property as is vested in the trustee, and if he fails to do so he shall be guilty of a contempt of court; and the court may also, if it thinks fit, revoke his discharge, but without prejudice to the validity of any sale, disposition or payment duly made or thing duly done subsequent to the discharge but before its revocation.
(*See Forms 81 to 90*)

Fraudulent settlements

31.   In either of the following cases, that is to say-

- (*a*)   in the case of a settlement made before and in consideration of marriage where the settlor is not at the time of making the settlement able to pay all his debts without the aid of the property comprised in the settlement; or

- (*b*)   in the case of any covenant or contract made in consideration of

marriage for the future settlement on or for the settlor's wife or children of any money or property wherein he had not at the date of his marriage any estate or interest (not being money or property of or in right of his wife),

if the settlor is adjudged bankrupt or compounds or arranges with his creditors and it appears to the court that such settlement, covenant or contract was made in order to defeat or delay creditors, or was unjustifiable having regard to the state of the settlor's affairs at the time when it was made, the court may refuse or suspend an order of discharge or grant an order subject to conditions or refuse to approve a composition or arrangement, as the case may be, in like manner as in cases where the debtor has been guilty of fraud.

Effect of order of discharge

32.(1) An order of discharge shall not release the bankrupt-

    (a)   from any debt on a recognizance nor from any debt with which the bankrupt may be chargeable at the suit of the Crown or of any person for any offence against a statute relating to any branch of the public revenue, or at the suit of any public officer on a bail bond entered into for the appearance of any person prosecuted for any such offence, and he shall not be discharged from such excepted debts unless the Financial Secretary certifies in writing his consent to his being discharged therefrom; or

    (aa)   from any liability to pay any amount under a confiscation order made under the Drug Trafficking (Recovery of Proceeds) Ordinance (Cap. 405) or under an external confiscation order registered under that Ordinance; or

    (b)   from any debt or liability incurred by means of any fraud or fraudulent breach of trust to which he was a party, or from any debt or liability whereof he has obtained forbearance by any fraud to which he was a party.

(2)   An order of discharge shall release the bankrupt from all other debts provable in bankruptcy.

(3)   An order of discharge shall be conclusive evidence of the bankruptcy and of the validity of the proceedings therein, and in any proceedings that may be instituted against a bankrupt who has obtained an order of discharge in respect of any debt from which he is released by the order, the bankrupt may plead that the cause of action occurred before his discharge.

(4)   An order of discharge shall not release any person who at the date of the receiving order was a partner or co-trustee with the bankrupt or was jointly bound or had made any joint contract with him, or any person who was surety or in the nature of a surety for him.

Power for court to annul adjudication in certain cases

33.(1) Where in the opinion of the court a debtor ought not to have been adjudged bankrupt, or where it is proved to the satisfaction of the court that the debts of the bankrupt are paid in full, the court may, on the application of any person interested, by order annul the adjudication.

(1A)   The court may, on the application of the Official Receiver, by order-

    (a)   rescind a receiving order made against a debtor; or

       (b)   annul an adjudication of bankruptcy made against a bankrupt, if the court is

satisfied that the assets for division among the unsecured creditors after payment of all costs, charges and expenses and the debts which are preferential under this Ordinance are not and will not be sufficient to pay a dividend of 15 per cent, and that it is desirable in all the circumstances of the case for such order to be made.

(2)   Where an order is made under this section rescinding a receiving order or annulling an adjudication, all sales and dispositions of property and payments duly made, and all acts theretofore done, by the Official Receiver, trustee or other person acting under their authority, or by the court, shall be valid, but the property of the debtor, if he has been adjudged bankrupt, shall vest in such person as the court may appoint, or in default of any such appointment revert to the debtor for all his estate or interest therein on such terms and subject to such conditions, if any, as the court may declare by order.

(3)   Notice of the order rescinding a receiving order or annulling an adjudication shall be forthwith gazetted and shall be advertised in at least 2 local newspapers, one of which shall be Chinese, or as may be prescribed.

(4)   For the purposes of this section, any debt disputed by a debtor shall be considered as paid in full if the debtor enters into a bond, in such sum and with such sureties as the court approves, to pay the amount to be recovered in any proceeding for the recovery of or concerning the debt, with costs, and any debt due to a creditor who cannot be found or cannot be identified shall be considered as paid in full if paid into court.

PART III - Administration Of Property

Proof of debts

Description of debts provable in bankruptcy

34.(1) Demands in the nature of unliquidated damages arising otherwise than by reason of a contract, promise or breach of trust shall not be provable in bankruptcy.

(2) A person having notice of any act of bankruptcy available against the debtor shall not prove in bankruptcy for any debt or liability contracted by the debtor subsequently to the date of his so having notice.

(3) Save as aforesaid, all debts and liabilities, present or future, certain or contingent, to which the debtor is subject at the date of the receiving order, or to which he may become subject before his discharge by reason of any obligation incurred before the date of the receiving order, including a liability to pay further damages as provided for in section 56A(2)(b) of the Supreme Court Ordinance (Cap. 4) (following an award of provisional damages), shall be deemed to be debts provable in bankruptcy.

(4) An estimate shall be made by the trustee of the value of any debt or liability provable as aforesaid which by reason of its being subject to any contingency or contingencies, or for any other reason, does not bear a certain value.

(5) Any person aggrieved by any estimate made by the trustee as aforesaid may appeal to the court.

(6) If in the opinion of the court the value of the debt or liability is incapable of being fairly estimated, the court may make an order to that effect, and thereupon the debt or liability shall, for the purposes of this Ordinance, be deemed to be a debt not provable in bankruptcy.

(7) If in the opinion of the court the value of the debt or liability is capable of being fairly estimated, the court may direct the value to be assessed before the court itself without the intervention of a jury and may give all necessary directions for this purpose, and the amount of the value when assessed shall be deemed to be a debt provable in bankruptcy.

(8) For the purposes of this Ordinance, "liability" includes-

      (a)   any compensation for work or labour done;

      (b)   any obligation or possibility of an obligation to pay money or money's worth on the breach of any express or implied covenant, contract, agreement or undertaking, whether the breach does or does not occur, or is or is not likely to occur or capable of occurring, before the discharge of the debtor;

(c) generally, any express or implied engagement, agreement or undertaking to pay or capable of resulting in the payment of money or money's worth, whether the payment is, as respects amount, fixed or unliquidated, as respects time, present or future, certain or dependent on any one contingency or on 2 or more contingencies, or, as to mode of valuation, capable of being ascertained by fixed rules or as matter of opinion.

Mutual credit and set-off

35. Where there have been mutual credits, mutual debts or other mutual dealings between a debtor against whom a receiving order is made under this Ordinance and any other person proving or claiming to prove a debt under the receiving order, an account shall be taken of what is due from the one party to the other in respect of such mutual dealings and the sum due from the one party shall be set off against any sum due from the other party and the balance of the account, and no more, shall be claimed or paid on either side respectively; but a person shall not be entitled under this section to claim the benefit of any set-off against the property of a debtor in any case where he had, at the time of giving credit to the debtor, notice of an act of bankruptcy committed by the debtor and available against him.

Rules as to proof of debts

36. The Chief Justice may, with the approval of the Legislative Council, make rules providing for the mode of proving debts, the right of proof by secured and other creditors, the admission and rejection of proofs, and other matters.

Priority of costs and charges

37.(1) The assets remaining after payment of the actual expenses incurred in realizing any of the assets of the debtor shall, subject to any order of the court, first be liable to the following payments, which shall be made in the following order of priority, namely-

    (a)   the actual expenses incurred by the Official Receiver in protecting or attempting to protect the property or assets of the debtor or any part thereof and any expenses or outlay incurred by him or by his authority in carrying on the business of the debtor;

    (b)   the fees, percentages and charges payable to, or costs, charges and expenses incurred or authorized by, the Official Receiver, whether acting as Official Receiver or trustee;

    (c)   the remuneration of the special manager, if any; and

    (d)   the taxed costs of the petitioner, so far as the same may not have been disallowed by the court.

(2)   Whenever the court is satisfied that property of a debtor in respect of whose estate a receiving order has been made has been preserved for the benefit of the creditors by means of legal proceedings brought by a creditor against the debtor without notice of any available act of bankruptcy committed by the debtor, the court may in its discretion order the payment of the costs of such legal proceedings or any part of them (taxed as between party and party) out of the estate, with the same priority as to payment as is herein provided in respect of the taxed costs of the petitioner.

Priority of debts

38.(1) In the distribution of the property of a bankrupt there shall be paid inpriority to all other debts-

    (a)   *(Repealed)*

    (b)   any-

        (i)   payment from the Protection of Wages on Insolvency Fund under section 18 of the Protection of Wages on Insolvency Ordinance (Cap. 380) to any clerk or servant in respect of wages or salary or both in respect of services rendered to the bankrupt if such payment was made during a period of 4 months before the date of the filing of the petition; and

        (ii)   wages and salary (including commission provided that the amount thereof is fixed or ascertainable at the relevant date) of any clerk or servant in respect of services rendered to the bankrupt during a period-

            (A)   beginning 4 months next before the date of the filing of the petition and ending on the making of the receiving order; or

            (B)   beginning 4 months next before the date of application for an *ex gratia* payment, under section 16 of the Protection of Wages on Insolvency Ordinance (Cap. 380), from the

                Protection of Wages on Insolvency Fund, and ending on that date of application, whichever is the earlier, not exceeding, together with any payment under sub-paragraph (i), $300;

    (c)   any-

(i) payment from the Protection of Wages on Insolvency Fund under section 18 of the Protection of Wages on Insolvency Ordinance (Cap. 380) to any labourer or workman in respect of wages, whether payable for time or for piece work, in respect of services rendered to the bankrupt if such payment was made during a period of 4 months before the date of the filing of the petition; and

(ii) wages of any labourer or workman, whether payable for time or for piece work, in respect of services rendered to the bankrupt during the period-

(A) beginning 4 months next before the date of the filing of the petition and ending on the making of the receiving order; or

(B) beginning 4 months next before the date of application for an ex gratia payment, under section 16 of the Protection of Wages on Insolvency Ordinance (Cap. 380), from the Protection of Wages on Insolvency Fund, and ending on that date of application,

whichever is the earlier, not exceeding, together with any payment under sub-paragraph (i), $100;

(ca) any severance payment payable to an employee under the Employment Ordinance (Cap. 57), not exceeding in respect of each employee $6,000;

(caa) any long service payment payable to an employee under the Employment Ordinance (Cap. 57), not exceeding in respect of each employee $8,000;

(cb) any amount due in respect of compensation or liability for compensation under the Employees' Compensation Ordinance (Cap. 282) accrued before the date of the receiving order and, where the compensation is a periodical payment, the amount due in respect thereof shall be taken to be the amount of the lump sum for which the periodical payment could, if redeemable, be redeemed on an application being made for that purpose under the Employees' Compensation Ordinance (Cap. 282), but this

paragraph shall not apply to any amount due in respect of compensation or liability for compensation where the bankrupt has entered into a contract with a person carrying on accident insurance business in Hong Kong in respect of his liability under the Employees' Compensation Ordinance (Cap. 282) for personal injury by accident to the employee to whom the compensation or liability for compensation is due;

(cc) any wages in lieu of notice payable to an employee under the Employment Ordinance (Cap. 57), not exceeding in respect of each employee one month's wages or $2,000 whichever is the lesser;

(cd) all accrued holiday remuneration becoming payable to any clerk, servant, workman or labourer (or in the case of his death to any o other person in his right) on the termination of his employment before or as a consequence of the receiving order;

(ce) any payment from the Employees Compensation Assistance Fund under Part IV of the Employees Compensation Assistance Ordinance (Cap. 365) representing an amount due by the bankrupt in respect of compensation or liability for compensation under the Employees' Compensation Ordinance (Cap. 282) accrued before the date of the receiving order;

(cf) any amount of unpaid contribution or any amount deemed to be unpaid contribution calculated in accordance with rules made under section 73(1)(n) of the Occupational Retirement Schemes Ordinance (Cap. 426) which should have been paid by the bankrupt in accordance with the terms of an occupational retirement scheme within the meaning of that Ordinance before the commencement of the bankruptcy:

Provided that where such amount exceeds $50,000 in respect of an employee, 50% of such part of the amount that exceeds $50,000 shall not be paid in priority to all other debts under this subsection;

(cg) (without prejudice to any right or liability under a trust) any amount of salaries deducted by the bankrupt from his employees' salaries for the purpose of making contributions in respect of such employees to the funds of an occupational retirement scheme within the meaning of the Occupational Retirement Schemes Ordinance (Cap. 426) which have not been paid into such funds;

(d) all statutory debts due from the bankrupt to the Crown at the date of the receiving order and which became due and payable within 12 months next before that date.

(2) Where the date of the receiving order is after 27 March 1953, but before 1 June 1970, the sum of $3,000 shall be deemed to be substituted in each case for the sums of $300 and $100 referred to respectively in subsection (1)(b) and(c).

(2A)   Where the date of the receiving order is on or after 1 June 1970, but before 1 April 1977, the sum of $6,000 shall be deemed to be substituted in each case for the sums of $300 and $100 referred to in subsection (1)(b) and (c) respectively.

(2B)   Where the date of the receiving order is on or after 1 April 1977, the sum of $8,000 shall be deemed to be substituted in each case for the sums of $300 and $100 referred to in paragraphs (b) and (c) respectively, and for the sum of $6,000 referred to in paragraph (ca), of subsection (1).

(3) The debts specified in subsection (1)(b), (c), (ca), (caa), (cb), (cc), (cd), (ce), (cf) and (cg) -

      (a)   shall have priority over the debts specified in subsection (1)(d);

      (b)   shall rank equally among themselves; and

      (c)   shall be paid in full unless the property of the bankrupt is insufficient to meet them, in which case they shall abate in equal proportions among themselves.

(3A)   *(Repealed)*

(4) Subject to the provisions contained in section 37 and to the retention of such sums as may be necessary for the costs of administration or otherwise, the foregoing debts shall be discharged forthwith so far as the property of the debtor is sufficient to meet them.

(5) In the event of a landlord or other person distraining or having distrained on any goods or effects of a bankrupt within 3 months next before the date of the receiving order the debts to which priority is given by this section shall be a first charge on the goods or effects so distrained on or the proceeds of the sale thereof.

(5A)   Any money paid under a charge under subsection (5) shall be a debt due from the estate of the bankrupt to the landlord or other person distraining or having distrained, and such debt shall be discharged so far as the property of the bankrupt is sufficient to meet it after payment of the debts specified in subsection (1) but before payment of the other debts proved in the bankruptcy.

(5B)   Where any assets have been recovered under an indemnity for costs of litigation given by certain creditors, or have been protected or preserved by the payment of moneys or the giving of indemnity by creditors, or where expenses in relation to which a creditor has indemnified a trustee have been recovered, the court may, on the application of the Official Receiver or the trustee or any such creditor, make such order as it deems just with respect to the distribution of those assets and the amount of those expenses so recovered with a view to giving those creditors an advantage over others in consideration of the risk run by them in so doing.

(5C) Any remuneration in respect of a period of holiday or of absence from work through sickness or other good cause shall be deemed to be wages in respect of services rendered to the bankrupt during that period.

(6) This section shall apply in the case of a deceased person who dies insolvent as if he were a bankrupt and as if the date of his death were substituted for the date of the receiving order.

(7) In the case of partners the joint estate shall be applicable in the firstinstance in payment of their joint debts and the separate estate of each partnershall be applicable in the first instance in payment of his separate debts. If thereis a surplus of the separate estates, it shall be dealt with as part of the joint estate. If there is a surplus of the joint estate, it shall be dealt with as part of the respective separate estates in proportion to the right and interest of each partner in the joint

estate. (*See Rule 195*)

(8) Subject to the provisions of this Ordinance, all debts proved in the bankruptcy shall be paid *pari passu.*

(9) If there is any surplus after payment of the foregoing debts, it shall be applied in payment of interest from the date of the receiving order at the rate of 8 per cent per annum on all debts proved in the bankruptcy.

(10) In this section-

"accrued holiday remuneration" includes, in relation to any person, all sums which, by virtue either of his contract of employment or of any enactment (including any order made or direction given under any Ordinance), are payable on account of the remuneration which would, in the ordinary course, have become payable to him in respect of a period of holiday had his employment with the bankrupt continued until he became entitled to be allowed the holiday;

"Employees Compensation Assistance Fund" means the fund established by section 7 of the Employees Compensation Assistance Ordinance (Cap.365);

"Protection of Wages on Insolvency Fund" means the fund deemed to be established and continued in existence under section 6 of the Protection of Wages on Insolvency Ordinance (Cap. 380);

"statutory debt" means a debt the liability for which and the amount of which are determined by or under any provision in any Ordinance or imperial enactment;

"wages" includes, in relation to any person, any sum which, by virtue of his contract of employment, is payable to him as a Lunar New Year bonus, but does not include any accrued holiday remuneration.

(11) The Bankruptcy (Amendment) Ordinance 1984 shall not apply in the case of a bankruptcy where the date of the receiving order occurred before the commencement of that Ordinance, and, in such a case, the provisions relating to priority of debts which would have applied if that Ordinance had not been enacted shall be deemed to remain in full force.

(12) The Fifth Schedule to the Protection of Wages on Insolvency Ordinance (Cap. 380) shall not apply in the case of a bankruptcy where the date of the filing of a petition occurred before the commencement of that Ordinance, and, in such case, the provisions relating to priority of debts which would have applied if that Ordinance had not been enacted shall be deemed to remain in full force.

Preferential claims in case of apprenticeship

39.(1) Where at the time of the presentation of the bankruptcy petition any person is apprenticed or is a trainee solicitor to the bankrupt, the adjudication of bankruptcy shall, if either the bankrupt or the apprentice or trainee solicitor gives notice in writing to the trustee to that effect, be a complete discharge of the indenture of apprenticeship or trainee solicitor contract; and if any money has been paid by or on behalf of the apprentice or trainee solicitor to the bankrupt as a fee, the trustee may, on the application of the apprentice or trainee solicitor or of some person on his behalf, pay such sum as the trustee, subject to an appeal to the court, thinks reasonable, out of the bankrupt's property, to or for the use of the apprentice or trainee solicitor, regard being had to the amount paid by him or on his behalf and to the time during which he served with the bankrupt under the indenture or trainee solicitor contract before the commencement of the bankruptcy and to the other circumstances of the case.

(2) Where it appears expedient to a trustee, he may, on the application of any apprentice or trainee solicitor to the bankrupt or any person acting on behalf of such apprentice or trainee solicitor, instead of acting under the provisions of subsection (1), transfer the indenture of apprenticeship or trainee solicitor contract to some other person.

Landlord's power of distress

40. The Landlord or other person to whom any rent is due from the bankruptmay, subject to the provisions of Part III of the Landlord and Tenant (Consolidation) Ordinance (Cap. 7), at any time either before or after the commencement of the bankruptcy, distrain upon the goods or effects of the bankrupt for the rent due to him from the bankrupt, with this limitation, that if such distress for rent be levied after the commencement of the bankruptcy, it shall be available only for 6 months' rent accrued due prior to the date of the order of adjudication and shall not be available for rent payable in respect of any period subsequent to the date when the distress was levied, but the landlord or other person to whom the rent may be due from the bankrupt may prove under the bankruptcy for the surplus due for which the distress may not have been available.

Postponement of husband's and wife's claims

41.(1) Where a married woman has been adjudged bankrupt, her husband shall not be entitled to claim any dividend as a creditor in respect of any money or other estate lent or entrusted by him to her until all claims of the other creditors of his wife for valuable consideration in money or money's worth have been satisfied.

(2) Where a debtor has been adjudged bankrupt, any money or other estate of his wife lent or entrusted by her to him shall be treated as assets of his estate, and the wife shall not be entitled to claim any dividend as a creditor in respect of any such money or other estate until all claims of the other creditors of the debtor for valuable consideration in money or money's worth have been satisfied.

(3) In this section "married woman" and "wife" include "concubine"

Property available for payment of debts

Relation back of trustee's title

42. The bankruptcy of a debtor, whether it takes place on the debtor's own petition or upon that of a creditor or creditors, shall be deemed to have relation back to, and to commence at, the time of the act of bankruptcy being committed on which a receiving order is made against him, or, if the bankrupt is proved to have committed more acts of bankruptcy than one, to have relation back to, and to commence at, the time of the first of the acts of bankruptcy proved to have been committed by the bankrupt within 3 months next preceding the date of the presentation of the bankruptcy petition, but no bankruptcy petition, receiving order or adjudication shall be rendered invalid by reason of any act of bankruptcy anterior to the debt of the petitioning creditor.

Description of bankrupt's property divisible amongst creditors

43. The property of the bankrupt divisible amongst his creditors, and in this Ordinance referred to as the property of the bankrupt, shall not comprise thefollowing particulars-

> *(a)* property held by the bankrupt on trust for any other person;

> *(b)* the tools (if any) of his trade and the necessary wearing apparel and bedding of himself and his family dependent on and residing with him, to a value, inclusive of tools and apparel and bedding, not exceeding $3,000 in the whole:

But it shall comprise the following particulars-

> (i) all such property as may belong to or be vested in the bankrupt at the commencement of the bankruptcy or may be acquired by or devolve on him before his discharge;

> (ii) the capacity to exercise and to take proceedings for exercising all such powers in or over or in respect of property as might have

been exercised by the bankrupt for his own benefit at the commencement of his bankruptcy or before his discharge;

(iii)   all goods being at the commencement of the bankruptcy in the possession, order or disposition of the bankrupt, in his trade or business, by the consent and permission of the true owner, under such circumstances that he is the reputed owner thereof:
Provided that things in action other than debts due or growing due to the bankrupt in the course of his trade or business shall not be deemed goods within the meaning of this section.

Provisions as to second bankruptcy

44.(1)   Where a second or subsequent receiving order is made against a bankrupt, or where an order is made for the administration in bankruptcy of the estate of a deceased bankrupt, then for the purposes of any proceedings consequent upon any such order the trustee in the last preceding bankruptcy shall be deemed to be a creditor in respect of any unsatisfied balance of the debts provable against the property of the bankrupt in that bankruptcy.

(2)   In the event of a second or subsequent receiving order made against a bankrupt being followed by an order adjudging him bankrupt, or in the event of an order being made for the administration in bankruptcy of the estate of a deceased bankrupt, any property acquired by him since he was last adjudged bankrupt, which at the date when the subsequent petition was presented had not been distributed amongst the creditors in such last preceding bankruptcy, shall subject to any disposition thereof made by the Official Receiver or trustee in that bankruptcy, without knowledge of the presentation of the subsequent petition, and subject to the provisions of section 52, vest in the trustee in the subsequent bankruptcy or administration in bankruptcy as the case may be.

(3)   Where the trustee in any bankruptcy receives notice of a subsequent petition in bankruptcy against the bankrupt or after his decease of a petition for the administration of his estate in bankruptcy, the trustee shall hold any property then in his possession which has been acquired by the bankrupt since he was adjudged bankrupt until the subsequent petition has been disposed of, and if on the subsequent petition an order of adjudication or an order for the administration of the estate in bankruptcy is made, he shall transfer all such property or the proceeds thereof (after deducting his costs and expenses) to the trustee in the subsequent bankruptcy or administration in bankruptcy, as the case may be.

Effect of bankruptcy on antecedent and other transactions

Restriction of rights of creditor under execution or attachment

45.(1) Where a creditor has issued execution against the property of a debtor or has attached any debt due to him, he shall not be entitled to retain the benefit of the execution or attachment against the trustee in bankruptcy of the debtor unless he had completed the execution or attachment before the date of the receiving order and before notice of the presentation of any bankruptcy petition by or against the debtor, or of the commission of any available act of bankruptcy by the debtor.

(2)   For the purposes of this Ordinance-

         (a)   an execution against goods is completed by seizure and sale or by the making of a charging order under section 20 of the Supreme Court Ordinance (Cap. 4);

         (b)   an attachment of a debt is completed by the receipt of the debt; and

         (c)   an execution against land is completed by seizure, by the appointment of a receiver, or by the making of a charging order under the said section 20.

(3)   An execution completed as aforesaid is not invalid by reason only of its being an act of bankruptcy, and a person who purchases the goods in good faith under a sale by the bailiff shall in all cases acquire a good title to them against the trustee in bankruptcy.

(4)   The rights conferred by this section on the trustee in relation to executions against the property of the debtor and attachment of debts due to the debtor may be set aside by the court in favour of the creditor to such extent and subject to such terms as the court may think fit.

Duties of bailiff as to goods taken in execution

46.(1) Where any movable property or negotiable instruments or money of a debtor are taken in execution, and before the receipt or recovery by the judgment creditor of the full amount of the levy, notice is served on the bailiff that a receiving order has been made against the debtor, the bailiff shall on request deliver the movable property, negotiable instruments or money, or any money received in satisfaction or part satisfaction of the execution, to the Official Receiver, but the costs of the execution shall be a first charge on the property so delivered and the Official Receiver or trustee may sell the movable property or negotiable instruments, or an adequate part thereof, or apply the money, for the purpose of satisfying the charge.

(2)   Where, under an execution in respect of a judgment for a sum exceeding $100, the property of a debtor is sold or money is paid in order to avoid sale, the bailiff shall deduct his costs of the execution from the proceeds of sale or the money paid and pay the balance into court, and if within 14 clear days of such sale or payment as aforesaid a bankruptcy petition is presented by or against the debtor, the said balance shall remain in court and if the debtor is adjudged bankrupt the balance shall be paid out to the trustee in the bankruptcy, who shall be entitled to retain the same as against the execution creditor, but otherwise it shall be dealt with as if no bankruptcy petition had been presented.

(3) The rights conferred by this section on the Official Receiver or trustee in relation to executions against any movable property or negotiable instruments or money of the debtor may be set aside by the court in favour of the creditor to such extent and subject to such terms as the court may think fit.

Avoidance of certain settlements

47.(1) Any settlement of property, not being a settlement made before and in consideration of marriage, or made in favour of a purchaser or incumbrancer in good faith and for valuable consideration, or a settlement made on or for the wife or children of the settlor of property which has accrued to the settlor after marriage in right of his wife, shall, if the settlor becomes bankrupt within 2 years after the date of the settlement, be void against the trustee in the bankruptcy, and shall, if the settlor becomes bankrupt at any subsequent time within 10 years after the date of the settlement, be void against the trustee in the bankruptcy, unless the parties claiming under the settlement can prove that the settlor was at the time of making the settlement able to pay all his debts without the aid of the property comprised in the settlement and that the interest of the settlor in such property passed to the trustee of such settlement on the execution thereof.

(2) Any covenant or contract made by any person (hereinafter called the settlor) in consideration of his or her marriage, either for the future payment of money for the benefit of the settlor's wife or husband or children or for the future settlement on or for the settlor's wife or husband or children of property, wherein the settlor had not at the date of the marriage any estate or interest, whether vested or contingent, in possession or remainder, and not being money or property in right of the settlor's wife or husband, shall if the settlor is adjudged bankrupt and the covenant or contract has not been executed at the date of the commencement of his bankruptcy, be void against the trustee in the bankruptcy except so far as it enables the persons entitled under the covenant or contract to claim for dividend in the settlor's bankruptcy under or in respect of the covenant or contract, but any such claim to dividend shall be postponed until all claims of the other creditors for valuable consideration in money or money's worth have been satisfied.

(3) Any payment of money (not being payment of premiums on a policy of life assurance), or any transfer of property made by the settlor in pursuance of such a covenant or contract as aforesaid, shall be void against the trustee in the settlor's bankruptcy unless the persons to whom the payment or transfer was made prove-

> *(a)* that the payment or transfer was made more than 2 years before the date of the commencement of the bankruptcy; or

> *(b)* that at the date of the payment or transfer the settlor was able to pay all his debts without the aid of the money so paid or the property so transferred;
> or
>
> *(c)* that the payment or transfer was made in pursuance of a covenant or contract to pay or transfer money or property expected to come to the settlor from or on the death of a particular person named in the covenant or contract and was made within 3 months after the money or property came into the possession or under the control of the settlor;

but, in the event of any such payment or transfer being declared void, the persons to whom it was made shall be entitled to claim for dividend under or in respect of the covenant or contract in like manner as if it had not been executed at the commencement of the bankruptcy.

(4)   For the purposes of this section, "settlement" includes any conveyance or transfer of property.

Avoidance of general assignments of book debts unless registered

48.(1) Where a person engaged in any trade or business makes an assignment to any other person of his existing or future book debts or any class thereof and is subsequently adjudicated bankrupt, the assignment shall be void against the trustee as regards any book debts which have not been paid at the commencement of the bankruptcy, unless the assignment has been registered with the Registrar in a register to be kept by him for that purpose:

Provided that nothing in this section shall have effect so as to render void any assignment of book debts due at the date of the assignment from specified debtors, or of debts growing due under specified contracts, or any assignment of book debts included in a transfer of a business made bona fide and for value, or in any assignment of assets for the benefit of creditors generally.

(2)   For the purposes of this section, "assignment" includes assignment by way of security and other charges on book debts.

Avoidance of preference in certain cases

49.(1) Every conveyance or transfer of property, or charge thereon made, every payment made, every obligation incurred and every judicial proceeding taken or suffered by any person unable to pay his debts as they become due from his own money in favour of any creditor or of any person in trust for any creditor, with a view to giving such creditor, or any surety or guarantor for the debt due to such creditor, a preference over the other creditors, shall, if the person making, taking, paying or suffering the same is adjudged bankrupt on a bankruptcy petition presented within 6 months, or in relation to anything made, taken, paid or suffered before the commencement of the Bankruptcy (Amendment) Ordinance 1984 3 months, after the date of making, taking, paying or suffering the same, be deemed fraudulent and void as against the trustee in the bankruptcy.

(2) This section shall not affect the rights of any person making title in good faith and for valuable consideration through or under a creditor of the bankrupt.

Liabilities and rights of certain fraudulently preferred persons

49A.(1) Where anything made or done after the commencement of the Bankruptcy (Amendment) Ordinance 1984 is void under section 49 as a fraudulent preference of a person interested in property mortgaged or charged to secure the debt, then (without prejudice to any rights or liabilities arising apart from this provision) the person preferred shall be subject to the same liabilities, and shall have the same rights, as if he had undertaken to be personally liable as surety for the debt to the extent of the charge on the property or the value of his interest, whichever is the less.

(2) The value of the said person's interest shall be determined as at the date of the transaction constituting the fraudulent preference, and shall be determined as if the interest were free of all incumbrances other than those to which the charge for the bankrupt's debt was then subject.

(3) On any application made to the court with respect to any payment on the ground that the payment was a fraudulent preference of a surety or guarantor, the court shall have jurisdiction to determine any questions with respect to the payment arising between the person to whom payment was made and the surety or guarantor and to grant relief in respect thereof, notwithstanding that it is not necessary so to do in respect of the bankruptcy and for that purpose may give leave to bring in the surety or guarantor as a third party as in the case of an action for the recovery of the sum paid.

(4) Subsection (3) shall apply, with the necessary modifications, in relation to transactions other than the payment of money as it applies in relation to payments.

Effects of lack of notice

50.(1) Subject to the provisions of this Ordinance with respect to the effect of bankruptcy on an execution or attachment and with respect to the avoidance of certain settlements, assignments and preferences, nothing in this Ordinance shall invalidate, in the case of a bankruptcy-

    (a) any payment by the bankrupt to any of his creditors;

    (b) any payment or delivery to the bankrupt;

    (c) any conveyance or assignment by the bankrupt for valuable consideration;

    (d) any contract, dealing or transaction by or with the bankrupt for valuable consideration:

Provided that both the following conditions are complied with, namely-

(i)   that the payment, delivery, conveyance, assignment, contract, dealing or transaction, as the case may be, takes place before the date of the receiving order; and

(ii)   that the person (other than the debtor) to, by or with whom the payment, delivery, conveyance, assignment, contract, dealing or transaction was made, executed or entered into has not at the time of the payment, delivery, conveyance, assignment, contract, dealing or transaction notice of any available act of bankruptcy committed by the bankrupt before that time.

(2)   Where any money or property of a bankrupt has, on or after the date of the receiving order but before notice thereof has been gazetted in the prescribed manner, been paid or transferred by a person having possession of it to some other person, and the payment or transfer is under the provisions of this Ordinance void as against the trustee in the bankruptcy, then if the person by whom the payment or transfer was made proves that when it was made he had not had notice of the receiving order, any right of recovery which the trustee may have against him in respect of the money or property shall not be enforced by any legal proceedings except where and in so far as the court is satisfied that it is not reasonably practicable for the trustee to recover in respect of the money or property or of some part thereof from the person to whom it was paid or transferred.

Validity of certain payments to bankrupt and assignee

51.   A payment of money or delivery of property to a person subsequently adjudged bankrupt or to a person claiming by assignment from him shall, notwithstanding anything in this Ordinance, be a good discharge to the person paying the money or delivering the property if the payment or delivery is made before the actual date on which the receiving order is made and without notice of the presentation of a bankruptcy petition, and is either pursuant to the ordinary course of business or otherwise bona fide.

Dealings with undischarged bankrupt

52.(1)   All transactions by a bankrupt with any person dealing with him bona fide and for value, in respect of property, whether leasehold or pure personalty, acquired by the bankrupt after the adjudication, shall, if completed before any intervention by the trustee, be valid against the trustee, and any estate or interest in such property which by virtue of this Ordinance is vested in the trustee shall determine and pass in such manner and to such extent as may be required for giving effect to any such transaction. For the purposes of this subsection, the receipt of any money, security or negotiable instrument from or by the order or direction of a bankrupt by his banker, and any payment and any delivery of any security or negotiable instrument made to or by the order or direction of a bankrupt by his banker, shall be deemed to be a transaction by the bankrupt with such banker dealing with him for value.

(2)   Where any individual, company or firm has ascertained that a person having a deposit, whether a deposit in respect of capital or not, or a credit balance, with such individual, company or firm is an undischarged bankrupt, then it shall be the duty of such individual, company or firm forthwith to inform the Official Receiver and the trustee in the bankruptcy of the existence of the deposit or credit balance, and such individual, company or firm shall not make any payment out of or in respect of the deposit or credit balance except under an order of the court or in accordance with instructions from the Official Receiver or the trustee in the bankruptcy.

(3) In case of any contravention of the provisions of subsection (2) the individual, or the directors and officers of the company, or the partners and manager of the firm, as the case may be, shall be liable on summary conviction to a fine of $1,000 and to imprisonment for 6 months.

Realization of property

Possession of property by trustee

53.(1) The trustee shall as soon as may be take possession of the deeds, books and documents of the bankrupt and all other parts of his property capable of manual delivery.

(2) The trustee shall, in relation to and for the purpose of acquiring or retaining possession of the property of the bankrupt, be in the same position as if he were a receiver of the property appointed by the court, and the court may on his application enforce such acquisition or retention accordingly.

(3) Where any part of the property of the bankrupt consists of stock, shares in ships, shares, or any other property transferable in the books of any company, office or person, the trustee may exercise the right to transfer the property to the same extent as the bankrupt might have exercised it if he had not become bankrupt.

(4) Where any part of the property of the bankrupt consists of things in action, such things shall be deemed to have been duly assigned to the trustee.

(5) Subject to the provisions of this Ordinance with respect to property acquired by a bankrupt after adjudication, any treasurer or other officer, or any banker, attorney, clerk, servant, comprador, employer or agent, of a bankrupt, shall pay and deliver to the trustee all money and securities in his possession or power, which he is not by law entitled to retain as against the bankrupt or the trustee. If he does not, he shall be guilty of a contempt of court and may be punished accordingly on the application of the trustee. (*See Forms 100, 103*)

Seizure of property of bankrupt

54. Any person acting under warrant of the court may seize any part of the property of a bankrupt, or of a debtor against whom a receiving order has been made, in the custody or possession of the bankrupt or the debtor or of any other person, and with a view to such seizure may break open any house, building or room of the bankrupt or the debtor where the bankrupt or the debtor is supposed to be, or any building or receptacle of the bankrupt or the debtor where any of his property is supposed to be; and where the court is satisfied that there is reason to believe that property of a bankrupt, or of a debtor against whom a receiving order has been made, is concealed in a house or place not belonging to him, the court may if it thinks fit grant a search warrant to any constable or officer of the court, who may execute it according to its tenor. (*See Form 108*)

Sale of property out of Hong Kong

55. Where the bankrupt is possessed of any property out of Hong Kong, thetrustee shall require him to join in selling the same for the benefit of the creditors and to sign all necessary authorities, powers, deeds and documents for the purpose, and if and so often as the bankrupt refuses to do so he may be punished for a contempt of court.

Appropriation of portion of pay, etc. to creditors

56.(1) Where a bankrupt is an officer of the navy, army or air force, or an officer or clerk or otherwise employed or engaged in the civil service of the Crown, or where a bankrupt is in receipt of any pay or pension from the Government or is entitled to any allowance or compensation granted by the Government, the trustee shall receive for distribution among the creditors so much of the bankrupt's pay, salary, pension, allowance or compensation as the court, with the consent of the Governor, on the application of the trustee, may direct. (*See Forms 118, 120*)

(2) Where a bankrupt is in receipt of a salary or income other than as aforesaid, the court, on the application of the trustee, may from time to time make such order as it thinks just for the payment of the salary or income or of any part thereof to the trustee, to be applied by him in such manner as the court may direct. (*See Form 121*)

(3) Nothing in this section shall take away or abridge any power to dismiss a bankrupt or to declare the pay, pension, allowance, compensation, salary or income of any bankrupt to be forfeited.

57. (*Repealed*)

Vesting and transfer of property

58.(1) Until a trustee is appointed the Official Receiver shall be the Trustee for the purposes of this Ordinance, and immediately on a debtor being adjudged bankrupt the property of the bankrupt shall vest in the trustee.

(2) On the appointment of a trustee the property shall forthwith pass to and vest in the trustee appointed.

(3) The property of the bankrupt shall pass from trustee to trustee, including under that term the Official Receiver when he fills the office of trustee, and shall vest in the trustee for the time being during his continuance in office, without any conveyance, assignment or transfer whatever.

Disclaimer of onerous property

59.(1) Where any part of the property of the bankrupt consists of land of any tenure burdened with onerous covenants, of shares or stock in companies, of unprofitable contracts, or of any other property that is unsaleable, or not readily saleable, by reason of its binding the possessor thereof to the performance of any onerous act or to the payment of any sum of money, the trustee, notwithstanding that he has endeavoured to sell or has taken possession of the property or exercised any act of ownership in relation thereto, but subject to the provisions of this section, may, by writing signed by him, at any time within 12 months after the first appointment of a trustee or such extended period as may be allowed by the court, disclaim the property:

Provided that, where any such property has not come to the knowledge of the trustee within 1 month after such appointment, he may disclaim such property at any time within 12 months after he has become aware thereof or such extended period as may be allowed by the court.

(2) The disclaimer shall operate to determine, as from the date of disclaimer, the rights, interests and liabilities of the bankrupt and his property in or in respect of the property disclaimed, and shall also discharge the trustee from all personal liability in respect of the property disclaimed as from the date when the property vested in him, but shall not, except so far as is necessary for the purpose of releasing the bankrupt and his property and the trustee from liability, affect the rights or liabilities of any other person.

(3) A trustee shall not be entitled to disclaim a lease without the leave of the court, except in any cases which may be prescribed by general rules, and the court may, before or on granting such leave, require such notices to be given to persons interested, and impose such terms as a condition of granting leave, and make such orders with respect to fixtures, tenant's improvements and other matters arising out of the tenancy, as the court thinks just.

(4) The trustee shall not be entitled to disclaim any property in pursuance of this section in any case where an application in writing has been made to the trustee by any person interested in the property requiring him to decide whether he will disclaim or not and the trustee has for a period of 28 days after the receipt of the application, or such extended period as may be allowed by the court, declined or neglected to give notice whether he disclaims the property or not; and in the case of a contract, if the trustee after such application as aforesaid does not within the said period or extended period disclaim the contract, he shall be deemed to have adopted it.

(5) The court may, on the application of any person who is, as against the trustee, entitled to the benefit or subject to the burden of a contract made with the bankrupt, make an order rescinding the contract on such terms as to payment by or to either party of damages for the non-performance of the contract, or otherwise, as to the court may seem equitable, and any damages payable under the order to any such person may be proved by him as a debt under the bankruptcy.

(6) The court may, on application by any person claiming either to have any interest in any disclaimed property or to be under any liability not discharged by this Ordinance in respect of any disclaimed property, and on hearing such persons as it thinks fit, make an order for the vesting of the property in or delivery thereof to any person entitled thereto, or to whom it may seem just that the same should be delivered by way of compensation for such liability as aforesaid, or a trustee for him, and on such terms as the court thinks just; and on any such vesting order being made, the property comprised therein shall vest accordingly in the person therein named in that behalf without any conveyance or assignment for the purpose:

Provided that where the property disclaimed is of a leasehold nature the court shall not make a vesting order in favour of any person claiming under the bankrupt, whether as under-lessee or as a person entitled to a mortgage except upon the terms of making that person-

> (a) subject to the same liabilities and obligations as the bankrupt was subject to under the lease in respect of the property at the date when the bankruptcy petition was filed; or
>
> (b) if the court thinks fit, subject only to the same liabilities and obligations as if the lease had been assigned to that person at that date,

and in either event (if the case so requires) subject only to the same liabilities and obligations as if the lease had comprised only the property comprised in the vesting order; and any under-lessee or person entitled to a mortgage who declines to accept a vesting order upon such terms shall be excluded from all interest in and security upon the property, and if there is no person claiming under the bankrupt who is willing to accept an order upon such terms, the court shall have power to vest the bankrupt's estate and interest in the property in any person liable either personally or in a representative character and either alone or jointly with the bankrupt to perform the lessee's covenants in the lease, freed and discharged from all estates, incumbrances and interests created there in by the bankrupt.

(7) Where on the release, removal, resignation or death of a trustee in bankruptcy the Official Receiver is acting as trustee, he may disclaim any property which might be disclaimed by a trustee under the foregoing provisions, notwithstanding that the time prescribed by this section for such disclaimer has expired, but such power of disclaimer shall be exercisable only within 12 months after the Official Receiver has become trustee in the circumstances aforesaid or has become aware of the existence of such property, whichever period may last expire.

(8) Any person injured by the operation of a disclaimer under this section shall be deemed to be a creditor of the bankrupt to the extent of the injury and may accordingly prove the same as a debt under the bankruptcy. (*See Forms 123 to 130*)

Powers of trustee to deal with property

60. Subject to the provisions of this Ordinance and to any order of the court, the trustee may do all or any of the following things-

> (a) sell all or any part of the property of the bankrupt (including the goodwill of the business, if any, and the book debts due or growing due to the bankrupt), by public auction or private

contract, with power to transfer the whole thereof to any person or company, or to sell the same in parcels, and any transfer of a business of a bankrupt by the Official Receiver or trustee shall be deemed to be exempted from the provisions of the Transfer of Businesses (Protection of Creditors) Ordinance (Cap. 49);

(b) give receipts for any money received by him, which receipts shall effectually discharge the person paying the money from all responsibility in respect of the application thereof,

(c) prove, rank, claim and draw a dividend in respect of any debt due to the bankrupt;

(d) exercise any powers the capacity to exercise which is vested in the trustee under this Ordinance and execute any powers of attorney, deeds and other instruments for the purpose of carrying into effect the provisions of this Ordinance.

Powers exercisable by trustee with permission of committee of inspection

61. The trustee may, with the permission of the committee of inspection, do all or any of the following things-

(a) carry on the business of the bankrupt so far as may be necessary for the beneficial winding up of the same;

(b) bring, institute or defend any action or other legal proceeding relating to the property of the bankrupt;

(c) employ a solicitor or other agent to take any proceedings or do any business which may be sanctioned by the committee of inspection;

(d) accept as the consideration for the sale of any property of the bankrupt a sum of money payable at a future time subject to such stipulations as to security and otherwise as the committee think fit;

(e) mortgage or pledge any part of the property of the bankrupt for the purpose of raising money for the payment of his debts;

(f) refer any dispute to arbitration, or compromise any debts, claims and liabilities, whether present or future, certain or contingent, liquidated or unliquidated, subsisting or supposed to

subsist between the bankrupt and any person who may have incurred any liability to the bankrupt, on the receipt of such sums, payable at such times and generally on such terms as may be agreed on;

(g)   make such compromise or other arrangement as may be thought expedient with creditors or persons claiming to be creditors in respect of any debts provable under the bankruptcy;

(h)   make such compromise or other arrangement as may be thought expedient with respect to any claim arising out of or incidental to the property of the bankrupt, made or capable of being made on the trustee by any person or by the trustee on any person;

(i)   divide in its existing form amongst the creditors, according to its estimated value, any property which from its peculiar nature or other special circumstances cannot be readily or advantageously sold.

The permission given for the purposes of this section shall not be a general permission to do all or any of the above-mentioned things but shall only be a permission to do the particular thing or things for which permission is sought in the specified case or cases.

Power to allow bankrupt to manage property

62. The trustee, with the permission of the committee of inspection, may appoint the bankrupt himself to superintend the management of the property of the bankrupt or of any part thereof, or to carry on the trade (if any) of the bankrupt for the benefit of his creditors, and in any other respect to aid in administering the property, in such manner and on such terms as the trustee may direct.

Allowance to bankrupt for maintenance or service

63. The trustee may from time to time, with the permission of the committee of inspection, make such allowance as he may think just to the bankrupt out of his property for the support of the bankrupt and his family, or in consideration of his services if he is engaged in winding up his estate, but any such allowance may be reduced by the court.

Right of trustee to inspect goods pawned, etc.

64. Where any goods of a debtor against whom a receiving order has been made are held by any person by way of pledge, pawn or other security, it shall be lawful for the Official Receiver or trustee, after giving notice in writing of his intention to do so, to inspect the goods, and where such notice has been given, such person as aforesaid shall not be entitled to realize his security until he has given the trustee a reasonable opportunity of inspecting the goods and of exercising his right of redemption if he thinks fit to do so.

Limitation of trustee's powers in relation to copyright

65. Where the property of a bankrupt comprises the copyright in any work or any interest in such copyright and he is liable to pay to the author of the work royalties or a share of the profits in respect thereof, the trustee shall not be entitled to sell or authorize the sale of any copies of the work, or to perform or authorize the performance of the work, except on the terns of paying to the author such sums by way of royalty or share of the profits as would have been payable by the bankrupt, nor shall he, without the consent of the author or of the court, be entitled to assign the right or transfer the interest or to grant any interest in the right by licence, except upon terms which will secure to the author payments by way of royalty or share of the profits at a rate not less than that which the bankrupt was liable to pay.

Protection of Official Receiver and trustee from personal liability in certain cases

66. Where the Official Receiver or trustee has seized or disposed of any goods, chattels, property or other effects in the possession or on the premises or under the control of a debtor against whom a receiving order has been made and it is thereafter made to appear that the said goods, chattels, property or other effects were not at the date of the receiving order the property of the debtor, the Official Receiver or trustee shall not be personally liable for any loss or damage arising from such seizure or disposal sustained by any person claiming such property nor for the costs of any proceedings taken to establish a claim thereto, unless the court is of opinion that the Official Receiver or trustee has been guilty of *mala fides* or of gross negligence in respect of the same.

Distribution of property
Declaration and distribution of dividends

67.(1) Subject to the retention of such sums as may be necessary for the costs of administration, or otherwise, the trustee shall with all convenient speed declare and distribute dividends amongst the creditors who have proved their debts.

(2) The first dividend, if any, shall be declared and distributed within 4 months after the conclusion of the first meeting of creditors, unless the trustee satisfies the court that there is sufficient reason for postponing the declaration to a later date.

(3) Subsequent dividends shall, in the absence of sufficient reason to the contrary, be declared and distributed at intervals of not more than 6 months.

(4) Before declaring a dividend, the trustee shall cause notice of his intention to do so to be gazetted and shall also send reasonable notice thereof to each creditor mentioned in the bankrupt's statement who has not proved his debt.

(5) When the trustee has declared a dividend he shall cause to be gazetted and shall send to each creditor who has proved a notice showing the amount of the dividend and when and how it is payable. (*See Forms 138, 139, 141*)

Joint and separate dividends

68.(1) Where one partner of a firm is adjudged bankrupt, a creditor to whom the bankrupt is indebted jointly with the other partners of the firm, or any of them, shall not receive any dividend out of the separate property of the bankrupt until all the separate creditors have received the full amount of their respective debts.

(2) Where joint and separate properties are being administered, dividends of the joint and separate properties shall, unless otherwise directed by the court on the application of any person interested, be declared together and the expenses of and incidental to such dividends shall be fairly apportioned by the trustee between the joint and separate properties, regard being had to the work done for and the benefit received by each property.

Provision for creditors residing at a distance, etc.

69.(1) In the calculation and distribution of a dividend the trustee shall make provision for debts provable in bankruptcy appearing from the bankrupt's statements, or otherwise, to be due to persons resident in places so distant from Hong Kong that in the ordinary course of communication they have not had sufficient time to tender their proofs or to establish them if disputed, and also for debts provable in bankruptcy the subject of claims not yet determined.

(2) He shall also make provision for any disputed proofs or claims, and for the expenses necessary for the administration of the estate or otherwise.

(3) Subject to the foregoing provisions, he shall distribute as dividend all money in hand.

Right of creditor who has not proved debt before declaration of a dividend

70. Any creditor who has not proved his debt before the declaration of any dividend or dividends shall be entitled to be paid out of any money for the time being in the hands of the trustee any dividend or dividends he may have failed to receive before that money is applied to the payment of any future dividend or dividends, but he shall not be entitled to disturb the distribution of any dividend declared before his debt was proved by reason that he has not participated therein.

Interest on debts

71.(1) Where a debt has been proved and the debt includes interest or any pecuniary consideration in lieu of interest, such interest or consideration shall, for the purposes of dividend, be calculated at a rate not exceeding 8 per cent per annum and be calculated only up to the date of the receiving order, without prejudice to the right of a creditor to receive out of the estate any higher rate of interest to which he may be entitled after all the debts proved in the estate have been paid in full.

(2) In dealing with the proof of the debt the following rules shall be

observed-

(a)   any account settled between the debtor and the creditor within 3 years preceding the date of the receiving order may be examined, and if it appears that the settlement of the account forms substantially one transaction with any debt alleged to be due out of the debtor's estate (whether in the form of renewal of a loan or capitalization of interest or ascertainment of loans or otherwise), the account may be reopened and the whole transaction treated as one;

(b)   any payments made by the debtor to the creditor before the receiving order, whether by way of bonus or otherwise, and any sums received by the creditor before the receiving order from the realization of any security for the debt shall, notwithstanding any agreement to the contrary, be appropriated to principal and interest in the proportion that the principal bears to the sum payable as interest at the agreed rate;

(c)   where the debt due is secured and the security is realized after the receiving order, or the value thereof is assessed in the proof, the amount realized or assessed shall be appropriated to the satisfaction of principal and interest in the proportion that the principal bears to the sum payable as interest at the agreed rate.

Final dividend

72.(1) When the trustee has realized all the property of the bankrupt, or so much thereof as can be realized without needlessly protracting the trusteeship, he shall declare a final dividend, but before so doing he shall give notice in manner prescribed to the persons whose claims to be creditors have been notified to him, but not established to his satisfaction, that if they do not establish their claims to the satisfaction of the court within a time limited by the notice, he will proceed to make a final dividend without regard to their claims.

(2) After the expiration of the time so limited or if the court on application by any such claimant grants him further time for establishing his claim, then on the expiration of such further time, the property of the bankrupt shall be divided among the creditors who have proved their debts, without regard to the claims of any other persons.

No action for dividend

73. No action for a dividend shall lie against the trustee, but if the trustee refuses to pay any dividend the court may, if it thinks fit, order him to pay it and also to pay out of his own money interest thereon for the time that it is withheld and the costs of the application.

Right of bankrupt to surplus

74.   The bankrupt shall be entitled to any surplus remaining after payment in full of his creditors, with interest, as by this Ordinance provided, and of the costs, charges and expenses of the proceedings under the bankruptcy petition.

PART III A - Criminal Bankruptcy

Interpretation

74A. In this Part and in Schedule 1-

"criminal bankruptcy administration petition" means a petition under section 112 presented by virtue of Schedule 1;

"criminal bankruptcy order" means an order made under section 84A of the Criminal Procedure Ordinance (Cap. 221);

"criminal bankruptcy petition" means a bankruptcy petition presented by virtue of Schedule 1.

Official Petitioner

Office and functions of Official Petitioner

74B.(1) For the purposes of discharging, in relation to cases in which a criminal bankruptcy order is made, the functions mentioned in subsection (2), there shall be an officer known as the Official Petitioner; and the Attorney General shall, by virtue of his office, be the Official Petitioner.

(2) The functions of the Official Petitioner shall be-

(a) to consider whether, in a case where a criminal bankruptcy order is made, it is in the public interest that he should himself present a criminal bankruptcy petition;

(b) to present a criminal bankruptcy petition in any such case where he determines it is in the public interest for him to do so;

(c) to make payments, in such cases as he may determine, towards expenses incurred by other persons in connexion with proceedings pursuant to a criminal bankruptcy petition or a criminal bankruptcy administration petition;

(d) to exercise, so far as he considers it to be in the public interest to do so, any of the powers conferred on him by Schedule 1.

(3) Neither the Official Petitioner nor any person acting under his authority shall be liable to any action or proceeding in respect of anything done or omitted in the discharge, or purported discharge, of the functions of the Official Petitioner under or by virtue of this Ordinance.

(4) Any functions of the Official Petitioner under this Ordinance may be discharged on his behalf by any person acting with his authority.

General

Effect of criminal bankruptcy order

74C.   Schedule 1 shall apply to give effect to the operation of this Ordinance in a case where a criminal bankruptcy order has been made and to supplement this Ordinance in relation to dispositions made by a person against whom such an order has been made.

PART IV - Official Receiver

Appointment of Official Receiver and other officers

75.(1) The Governor may appoint an Official Receiver and such other officers to hold any of the offices specified in Schedule 2 as may be required to assist the Official Receiver in the performance of his duties.

(2) No person shall be appointed Official Receiver or to any of the offices specified in Part I of Schedule 2 unless on the date of such appointment he is qualified to practise as a legal practitioner in Hong Kong, the United Kingdom or in a jurisdiction listed in Schedule 1 to the Legal Practitioners Ordinance (Cap. 159).

(3) The Official Receiver and the holder of an office specified in Part I of Schedule 2 shall be deemed to be legal officers for the purpose of the Legal Officers Ordinance (Cap. 87) and shall have all rights conferred upon legal officers by that Ordinance.

(4) The holder of an office specified in Schedule 2 may, subject to subsection (5) and any instructions of the Official Receiver, exercise the powers or perform the duties of the office of the Official Receiver.

(5) The holder of an office specified in Part II of Schedule 2 shall not exercise any right conferred by subsection (3) on the holder of an office specified in Part I of Schedule 2.

(6) The Official Receiver shall act under the general authority and direction of the Governor and shall also be an officer of the court.

(7) The Governor may, by order published in the Gazette, amend Schedule 2.

Status of Official Receiver

76.(1) The duties of the Official Receiver shall have relation both to the conduct of the debtor and to the administration of his estate.

(2) The Official Receiver and the holder of an office specified in Schedule 2 may take any affidavit required by any Ordinance to be made before or produced or delivered to or filed with the Official Receiver or the holder of an office specified in Schedule 2 notwithstanding any Ordinance requiring the taking of such affidavit by or before any other person.

(3) All provisions in this or any other Ordinance referring to the trustee in a bankruptcy shall, unless the context otherwise requires or the Ordinance otherwise provides, include the Official Receiver when acting as trustee.

(4) The trustee shall supply the Official Receiver with such information, and give him such access to and facilities for inspecting the bankrupt's books and documents, and generally shall give him such aid, as may be requisite for enabling the Official Receiver to perform his duties under this Ordinance.

Transitional provision

76A.(1) Any thing done before the commencement of the Bankruptcy (Amendment) Ordinance 1992 by the Registrar General in the capacity of Official Receiver shall be regarded as having been done by the Official Receiver at the time when the thing was done.

(2) Any document which contains a reference to the Registrar General in the capacity of Official Receiver shall have effect on and after the commencement of the Bankruptcy (Amendment) Ordinance 1992 with the substitution for such reference of a reference to the Official Receiver.

(3) In any legal proceedings pending on the commencement of the Bankruptcy (Amendment) Ordinance 1992 to which the Registrar General in the capacity of Official Receiver is a party, the Official Receiver shall as from such commencement be substituted as a party thereto in lieu of the Registrar General and the proceedings shall continue as if the Official Receiver had always been that party.

(4) In this section, "Registrar General" means the Registrar General appointed under section 2(1) of the Registrar General (Establishment) Ordinance (Cap. 100)T.

Duties of Official Receiver as regards the debtor's conduct

77. As regards the debtor, it shall be the duty of the Official Receiver-

(a)   to investigate the conduct of the debtor and to report to the court, stating whether there is reason to believe that the debtor has committed any act which constitutes an indictable offence under this Ordinance or which would justify the court in refusing, suspending or qualifying an order for his discharge;

(b)   to conduct the public examination of the debtor;

(c)   to take such part and give such assistance in relation to the prosecution of any fraudulent debtor as the Attorney General may direct.

Duties of Official Receiver as to debtor's estate

78.(1) As regards the estate of a debtor, it shall be the duty of the Official Receiver-

(a)   pending the appointment of a trustee, to act as interim receiver

of the debtor's estate, and where a special manager is not appointed, as manager thereof;

(b)   to raise money in any case where in the interests of the creditors it appears necessary so to do;

(c)   to summon and preside at the first meeting of creditors;

(d)   to issue forms of proxy for use at the meetings of creditors; (*See Forms 50, 51*)

(e)   to report to the creditors as to any proposal which the debtor may have made with respect to the mode of liquidating his affairs;

(f)   to advertise the receiving order, the date of the creditors' first meeting and of the debtor's public examination, and such other matters as it may be necessary to advertise; (*See Form 27*)

(g)   to act as trustee during any vacancy in the office of trustee;

(h)   to assist the debtor in preparing his statement of affairs in case the debtor has no solicitor acting for him and is unable properly to prepare it himself, and for this purpose he may employ at the expense of the estate any person or persons to assist in its preparation.

(2) For the purpose of his duties as interim receiver or manager the Official Receiver shall have the same powers as if he were a receiver and manager appointed by the court, but shall, as far as practicable, consult the wishes of the creditors with respect to the management of the debtor's property, and may for that purpose, if he thinks it advisable, summon meetings of the persons claiming to be creditors, and shall not, unless the court otherwise orders, incur any expense beyond such as is requisite for the protection of the debtor's property or the disposing of perishable goods.

(3) The Official Receiver shall account to the court and pay over all moneys and deal with all securities in such manner as the court from time to time directs.

PART V - Trustees In Bankruptcy

Official name

Official name of trustee

79. The official name of a trustee in bankruptcy shall be "the trustee of the property of a bankrupt" (inserting the name of thebankrupt), and by that name the trustee may hold property of every description, make contracts, sue and be sued, enter into any engagements binding on himself and his successors in office, and do all other acts necessary or expedient to be done in the execution of his office.

Appointment

Disqualification for appointment as trustee

79A. No person being an undischarged bankrupt and no body corporate shall be qualified for appointment to the office of trustee, and-

> *(a)* any appointment made in contravention of this section shall be void; and

> *(b)* where any such person or any body corporate acts as trustee, such person or body corporate shall be liable to a fine of $5,000.

Corrupt inducement affecting appointment as trustee

79B. Any person who gives or agrees or offers to give to any creditor of a debtor or bankrupt any valuable consideration with a view to securing his own appointment or nomination, or to securing or preventing the appointment or nomination of some person other than himself, as the trustee shall be liable to afine of $5,000.

Power to appoint joint or successive trustees

80.(1) The creditors may, if they think fit, appoint more persons than one to the office of trustee and, when more persons than one are appointed, shall declare whether any act required or authorized to be done by the trustee is to be done by all or any one or more of such persons, but all such persons are in this Ordinance included under the term "trustee" and shall be joint tenants of the property of the bankrupt.

(2) The creditors may also appoint persons to act as trustees in succession in the event of one or more of the persons first named declining to accept the office of trustee or failing to give security, or of the appointment of any such person not being approved by the court.

Proceedings in case of vacancy in office of trustee

81.(1) If a vacancy occurs in the office of a trustee the creditors in general meeting may appoint a person to fill the vacancy and thereupon the same proceedings shall be taken as in the case of a first appointment.

(2) The Official Receiver shall, on the requisition of any creditor, summon a meeting for the purpose of filling any such vacancy.

(3) If the creditors do not within 3 weeks after the occurrence of a vacancy appoint a person to fill the vacancy, the Official Receiver shall report the matter to the court, and the court may appoint a trustee.

(4) During any vacancy in the office of trustee the Official Receiver shall act as trustee.

Control over trustee

Discretionary powers of trustee and control thereof

82.(1) Subject to the provisions of this Ordinance, the trustee shall, in the administration of the property of the bankrupt and in the distribution thereof amongst his creditors, have regard to any directions that may be given by resolution of the creditors at any general meeting or by the committee of inspection, and any directions so given by the creditors at any general meeting shall, in case of conflict, be deemed to override any directions given by the committee of inspection.

(2) The trustee may from time to time summon general meetings of the creditors for the purpose of ascertaining their wishes, and it shall be his duty to summon meetings at such times as the creditors, by resolution, either at the meeting appointing the trustee or otherwise may direct, and it shall be lawful for any creditor, with the concurrence of one-fourth in value of the creditors (including himself), at any time to request the trustee or Official Receiver to call a meeting of the creditors, and the trustee or Official Receiver shall call such meeting accordingly within 14 days:

Provided that the person at whose instance the meeting is summoned shall, if so required, deposit with the trustee or the Official Receiver, as the case may be, a sum sufficient to pay the costs of summoning the meeting, such sum to be repaid to him out of the estate if the court so directs.

(3) The trustee may apply to the court in manner prescribed for directions in relation to any particular matter arising under the bankruptcy. (*See Forms 131, 132*)

(4) Subject to the provisions of this Ordinance the trustee shall use his discretion in the management of the estate and its distribution among the creditors.

Appeal to court against trustee

83. f the bankrupt or any of the creditors or any other person is aggrieved by any act or decision of the trustee, he may apply to the court, and the court may confirm, reverse or modify the act or decision complained of, and make such order in the premises as it thinks just.

Control of court over trustee

84.(1) The court shall take cognizance of the conduct of trustees, and in the event of any trustee not faithfully performing his duties and duly observing all the requirements imposed on him by Ordinance, rules or otherwise with respect to the performance of his duties, or in the event of any complaint being made to the court by any creditor in regard thereto by notice duly served on the trustee at least 8 clear days before the date of hearing, the court shall inquire into the matter and take such action thereon as may be deemed expedient.

(2) The court may either of its own motion or on the application of the Official Receiver at any time require any trustee to answer any inquiry made by it or him in relation to any bankruptcy in which the trustee is engaged and may examine on oath the trustee or any other person concerning the bankruptcy.

(3) The court may also direct an investigation to be made of the books and vouchers of the trustee.

Remuneration and costs
Remuneration of trustee

85.(1) Where the creditors appoint any person to be trustee of a debtor's estate, his remuneration (if any) shall be fixed by an ordinary resolution of the creditors, or, if the creditors so resolve, by the committee of inspection.

(2) Where the remuneration of the trustee is to be a commission upon the amount received by the trustee, then one part shall be payable on the amount realized by the trustee, after deducting any sums paid to secured creditors out of the proceeds of their securities, and the other part on the amount distributed in dividend.

(3) If one-fourth in number or value of the creditors apply to the Official Receiver or the Official Receiver is of the opinion that the remuneration of a trustee should be reviewed, the Official Receiver may apply to the court and thereupon the court may confirm, increase or reduce the remuneration of the trustee.

(4) The resolution or the committee of inspection, as the case may be, shall specify the expenses which the remuneration is to cover, and no liability shall attach to the bankrupt's estate, or to the creditors, in respect of any such expenses.

(5) Where a trustee acts without remuneration he shall be allowed out of the bankrupt's estate such proper expenses incurred by him in or about the proceedings of the bankruptcy as the court may approve.

(6) A trustee shall not under any circumstances whatever make any arrangement for or accept from the bankrupt, or any solicitor, auctioneer or any other person who may be employed about a bankruptcy, any gift, remuneration or pecuniary or other consideration or benefit whatever beyond his said remuneration payable out of the estate, nor shall he make any arrangement for giving up, or give up, any part of his remuneration, whether as receiver, manager or trustee, to the bankrupt or any solicitor or other person who may be employed about a bankruptcy.

Allowance and taxation of costs

86.(1) Where a trustee or manager receives remuneration for his services as such, no payment shall be allowed in his accounts in respect of the performance by any other person of the ordinary duties which are required by Ordinance or rules to be performed by himself.

(2) Where the trustee is a solicitor he may contract that the remuneration for his services as trustee shall include all professional services.

(3) All bills and charges of solicitors, managers, accountants, auctioneers, brokers and other persons, not being trustees, shall be taxed by the Registrar and no payments in respect thereof shall be allowed in the trustee's accounts without proof of such taxation having been made. The Registrar shall satisfy himself before passing such bills and charges that the employment of such solicitors and other persons, in respect of the particular matters out of which such charges arise, has been duly sanctioned. The sanction must be obtained before the employment, except in cases of urgency, and in such cases it must be shown that no undue delay took place in obtaining the sanction.

(4) Every such person shall, on request by the trustee (which request the trustee shall make a sufficient time before declaring a dividend), deliver his bill of costs or charges to the Registrar for taxation, and if he fails to do so within 7 days after receipt of the request or such further time as the court on application may grant, the trustee shall declare and distribute the dividend without regard to any claim by him, and thereupon any such claim shall be forfeited as well against the trustee personally as against the estate.

Receipts, payments, accounts, audit

Trustee to furnish list of creditors

87. The trustee or Official Receiver shall, whenever required by any creditor so to do, furnish and transmit to him by post a list of the creditors showing the amount of the debt due to each creditor, and shall be entitled to charge for such list the sum of 25 cents per folio of 72 words.

Trustee to furnish statement of accounts

88. It shall be lawful for any creditor, with the concurrence of one-fourth of the creditors (including himself), at any time to call upon the trustee or Official Receiver to furnish and transmit to the creditors a statement of the accounts up to the date of such notice, and the trustee shall upon receipt of such notice furnish and transmit such statement of the accounts: (*See Form 150*)

Provided that the person at whose instance the accounts are furnished shall, if so required, deposit with the trustee or Official Receiver, as the case may be, a sum sufficient to pay the costs of furnishing and transmitting the accounts, which sum shall be repaid to him out of the estate if the court so directs.

Annual statement of proceedings

89.(1) Every trustee in a bankruptcy shall from time to time, as may be prescribed, and not less than once in every year during the continuance of the bankruptcy, transmit to the Official Receiver a statement showing the proceedings in the bankruptcy up to the date of the statement, containing the prescribed particulars and made out in the prescribed form.

(2) The Official Receiver shall cause the statements so transmitted to be examined, and shall call the trustee to account for any misfeasance, neglect or omission which may appear on the said statements or in his accounts or otherwise, and may apply to the court for an order that the trustee do make good any loss which the estate of the bankrupt may have sustained by the misfeasance, neglect or omission.

Trustee not to pay into private account

90. No trustee in a bankruptcy or under any composition or scheme of arrangement shall pay any sums received by him as trustee into his private banking account or use them otherwise than in the administration of the estate.

Payment of moneys into bank

91.(1) The Official Receiver shall open in his name as Official Receiver an account at a bank approved by the Governor and shall pay to the credit thereof all sums received by him as such Official Receiver or as trustee, and every trustee in a bankruptcy, other than the Official Receiver, receiving money as such trustee shall open an account at such bank in the name of the debtor's estate and shall pay to the credit of such account all sums which may from time to time be received by him as such trustee:

Provided that the Official Receiver may, on the application of the committee of inspection, authorize any other trustee to make his payments into and out of any other bank specified by the committee in such application, and those payments shall be made in the prescribed manner.

(2) If a trustee at any time retains for more than 10 days a sum exceeding $2,000, or such other amount as the Official Receiver in any particular case may authorize him to retain, then unless he explains the retention to the satisfaction of the Official Receiver, he shall pay interest on the amount so retained in excess at the rate of 20 per cent per annum, and shall have no claim to remuneration, and may be removed from his office by the Official Receiver and shall be liable to pay any expenses occasioned by reason of his default.

(3) Any trustee paying money into his private banking account or using it otherwise than in the administration of the estate may without prejudice to any other liability be dismissed from office without remuneration and may be ordered by the court to make good all losses and expenses which the creditors may suffer in consequence of his conduct.

Record and account to be kept by trustee

92.(1) The trustee shall keep a record in writing in which he shall enter a minute of all proceedings had and resolutions passed at any meeting of creditors or of the committee of inspection and a statement of all negotiations and proceedings necessary to give a correct view of the management of the bankrupt's property. Such record if in Chinese shall be supplemented by a correct English translation thereof and shall be produced for inspection to the Official Receiver at any time on demand.

(2) The trustee shall also keep an account, to be called the estate account, in the form of an ordinary debtor and creditor account, in which he shall enter from day to day all his receipts and payments as trustee.

(3) The trustee shall produce at every meeting of creditors and at every meeting of the committee of inspection the record and account above-mentioned and also the pass-book of the estate's bank account, and such documents shall be open to the inspection of any creditor at all reasonable times.

Audit of trustee's accounts

93.(1) Every trustee other than the Official Receiver shall, at such times as may be prescribed but not less than once in each year during his tenure of office, send to the Official Receiver an account of his receipts and payments as such trustee.

(2) The account shall be in a prescribed form, shall be made in duplicate and shall be verified by an affidavit in the prescribed form. (*See Form 146*)

(3) The trustee shall furnish the Official Receiver with such vouchers and information relating to the account as he requires, and the Official Receiver may at any time require the production of, and inspect, any books or accounts kept by the trustee.

(3A) The Official Receiver may at any time cause the account to be audited.

(4) When any such account has been audited (or, as the case may be, forthwith if the Official Receiver decides that the account need not be audited) one copy thereof shall be filed and kept by the Official Receiver, and the other copy shall be delivered to the court for filing, and each copy shall be open on payment of the prescribed fee to the inspection of any creditor or of the bankrupt or of any person interested.

(4A)   Notwithstanding the fact that unaudited copies of an account have already been filed, the Official Receiver may subsequently cause that account to be audited, and in that event a copy of the audited account shall be filed and kept by the Official Receiver, and a further copy shall be delivered to the court for filing, and each copy shall be open, upon payment of the prescribed fee, to the inspection of any creditor or of the bankrupt or of any person interested.

(5) The court may if it so desires examine the trustee and, after hearing the explanation, if any, of the trustee, make such order as it may think just for compelling the trustee to make good any loss to the estate which may appear to the court to have been occasioned by any misfeasance, neglect or improper conduct or omission of the trustee.

Vacation of office by trustee
Release of trustee

94.(1) When the trustee has realized all the property of the bankrupt or so much thereof as can, in his opinion, be realized without needlessly protracting the trusteeship, and distributed a final dividend, if any, or has ceased to act by reason of a composition having been approved, or has resigned or has been removed from his office, he shall apply to the court for his release, and if all the requirements of the court with respect to accounts and with respect to any order of the court against the trustee have been fulfilled, the court may make an order for release accordingly.

(*See Forms 137, 152, 153*)

(2) Where the release of a trustee is withheld the court may, on the application of any creditor or person interested, make such order as it thinks just, charging the trustee with the consequences of any act or default he may have done or made contrary to his duty.

(3) An order of the court releasing the trustee shall discharge him from all liability in respect of any act done or default made by him in the administration of the affairs of the bankrupt, or otherwise in relation to his conduct as trustee, but any such order may be revoked on proof that it was obtained by fraud or by suppression or concealment of any material fact.

(4) The provisions of subsections (1), (2) and (3) shall apply to the Official Receiver when he is or is acting as trustee, and when the Official Receiver has been released under this section or any previous similar enactment he shall continue to act as trustee for any subsequent purposes of the administration of the debtor's estate but no liability shall attach to him personally by reason of his so continuing in respect of any act done, default made or liability incurred before his release.

(5) Where the trustee has not previously resigned or been removed, his release shall operate as a removal of him from his office, and thereupon the Official Receiver shall be the trustee.

(6) Where on the release of a trustee the Official Receiver is or is acting as trustee, no liability shall attach to him personally in respect of any act done or default made or liability incurred by any prior trustee.

Office of trustee vacated by insolvency

95. If a receiving order is made against a trustee he shall thereby vacate his office of trustee.

Removal of trustee

96.(1) The creditors may by ordinary resolution, at a meeting specially called for that purpose of which 7 days' notice has been given, remove a trustee, other than the Official Receiver, appointed by them, and may at the same or any subsequent meeting appoint another person to fill the vacancy as provided in case of a vacancy in the office of trustee.

(2)   If the court is of opinion-

    (a)   that a trustee appointed by the creditors is guilty of misconduct or fails to perform his duties under this Ordinance; or

    (b)   that his trusteeship is being needlessly protracted without any probable advantage to the creditors; or

    (c)   that he is by reason of lunacy or continued sickness or absence incapable of performing his duties; or

    (d)   that his connexion with or relation to the bankrupt or his estate or any particular creditor might make it difficult for him to act with impartiality in the interest of the creditors generally; or

    (e)   that the interests of the creditors require it,

the court may remove him from his office and appoint another person in his place.

PART VI - Constitution, Procedure And Powers Of Court

Jurisdiction

General power of court

97.(1) Subject to the provisions of this Ordinance, the court shall have full power todecide all questions of priorities and all other questions whatsoever, whether of law or fact, which may arise in any case of bankruptcy coming within the cognizance of the court or which the court may deem it expedient or necessary to decide for the purpose of doing complete justice or making a complete distribution of property in any such case.

(2) If in any proceeding in bankruptcy there arises any question of fact which either of the parties desires to be tried before a jury instead of by the court itself or which the court thinks ought to be tried by a jury, the court may, if it thinks fit, direct the trial to be had with a jury and the trial may be had accordingly. (*See Form 133*)

Review and appeals

Review and appeals in bankruptcy

98.(1) The court or the Registrar may review, rescind or vary any order made by it or him, as the case may be, under its or his bankruptcy jurisdiction.

(2) Every order of the court or the Registrar shall be subject to appeal to the Court of Appeal. The appeal shall be commenced within 21 days from the time when the decision appealed against is pronounced or made.

Procedure

General rules of procedure

99.(1) The rules and practice of the Supreme Court for the time being for regulating the ordinary civil procedure of the court shall, so far as the same may be applicable and not inconsistent with the provisions of this Ordinance, be applied to bankruptcy proceedings, and every order of the court made in connexion with bankruptcy proceedings may be enforced in the same way as a judgment of the court made in respect of any other civil proceedings may be enforced.

(2) The Registrar shall in cases of urgency have power to make interim orders and to hear and determine unopposed or *ex parte* applications and any order so made shall, subject to an appeal to the court, be deemed to be an order of the court.

(3) Subject to rules made under section 113 limiting the power conferred by thissubsection, the Registrar sitting in open court shall have power to hear and determine-

> *(a)*   unopposed bankruptcy petitions and to make receiving orders thereon;
>
> *(b)*   applications to rescind receiving orders or to annul an adjudication;
>
> *(c)*   applications to approve compositions or schemes of arrangement; and
>
> *(d)*   applications for orders of discharge.

Jurisdiction of Registrar

99A.(1)   Unless otherwise ordered by the court in a particular case, the Registrar may exercise and perform the powers and duties conferred or imposed upon the court by sections 19 and 29.

(2)   The Registrar may, if he exercises the jurisdiction conferred on him by subsection (1) or section 99(3) -

> *(a)*   refer any matter for the decision or direction of a judge; and
>
> *(b)*   at any time adjourn an examination for further hearing before a judge.

(3) A judge may, if a matter is referred to him under subsection (2)(a), dispose of it himself or refer it back to the Registrar with such directions as he thinks fit.

(4) A judge may, if an examination is adjourned under subsection (2)(b) for further hearing before a judge-

> *(a)*   continue the examination;
>
> *(b)*   at any time direct that the examination be continued before the Registrar; and
>
> *(c)*   make such other order and give such directions as he may consider proper.

(5) Any reference in this Ordinance to the court shall include a reference to the Registrar exercising the jurisdiction conferred on him by this section.

(6) Notwithstanding subsection (5), the Registrar, when exercising the jurisdiction conferred by this section, shall not have power to make an order for the committal of a person for contempt of court.

(7) In this section-

"Registrar" means-

    (a)   the Registrar of the Supreme Court;

    (b)   any Deputy Registrar of the Supreme Court; and

    (c)   any Assistant Registrar of the Supreme Court appointed by the Chief Justice for the purposes of this section.

Discretionary powers of court

100.(1) Subject to the provisions of this Ordinance and to general rules, the costs of and incidental to any proceeding in court under this Ordinance shall be in the discretion of the court:

Provided that, where any issue is tried by a jury, the costs shall follow the event unless, upon application made at the trial, for good cause shown, the judge before whom such issue is tried otherwise orders.

(2) The court may at any time adjourn any proceedings before it upon terms, if any, as it may think fit to impose.

(3) The court may at any time amend any written process or proceeding under this Ordinance upon such terms, if any, as it may think fit to impose.

(4) Where by this Ordinance or by general rules the time for doing any act or thing is limited, the court may extend the time either before or after the expiration thereof upon such terms, if any, as the court may think fit to impose.

(5) Subject to general rules, the court may in any matter take the whole or any part of the evidence viva voce or by interrogatories or upon affidavit or, out of Hong Kong, by commission.

Court may make a regulating order

100A.(1 Where it appears to the court on application being made by the Official Receiver or by any creditor at any time after the presentation of a bankruptcy petition, whether presented before or after the commencement of the Bankruptcy (Amendment) Ordinance 1965, that by reason of the large number of creditors or for any other reason the interest of the creditors so requires, it may, on or after the making of a receiving order, order that the bankruptcy proceedings shall be regulated specially by the court, and such order shall be known as a regulating order.

(2) A regulating order shall be published in such manner as the court may direct, and sections 100B to 100H inclusive shall apply to the bankruptcy proceedings where a regulating order has been made but not otherwise.

(3) Where a regulating order is made the Bankruptcy Rules (Cap. 6 sub. leg.) shall apply *mutatis mutants* to the Official Receiver, trustee and committee of inspection appointed or acting after the making of a regulating order, and to the conduct of any ballot or other proceedings ordered by the court under section 100B or 100F.

(4) Where any order made under sections 100B to 100G inclusive prescribes any procedure it shall be deemed to be in substitution for the procedure which would be required by this Ordinance but for the making of such order, and in particular where any such order prescribes a procedure for doing something which would otherwise be done at a meeting of creditors no such meeting shall be required to be held.

First meeting and composition

100B.(1) The court may on the application of the Official Receiver by order dispense with the summoning of the first meeting of creditors required under section 17.

(2) The court may order that the wishes of creditors be ascertained for thepurpose of accepting or rejecting any composition in such manner as it may direct without the holding of meetings under section 20 or 25, and for such purpose may direct the manner in which any composition be communicated to such creditors.

(3) Without derogating from the generality of subsection (2) the court may direct the holding of a ballot and the use of voting letters.

(4) Notwithstanding anything in section 20 or 25, where a majority in number and three-fourths in value of all the creditors who have proved their debt, or who by virtue of section 100H are deemed for voting purposes to have proved a debt exceeding $100, agree to accept a composition, the composition shall be deemed to be duly accepted by the creditors, and when approved by the court shall be binding on all the creditors.

(5) For the purposes of this section and section 100C, "composition" means any proposal for a composition in satisfaction of the debts of the debtor or for any scheme of arrangement of the affairs of the debtor.

Adjudication

100C.(1) The court shall on application being made by the Official Receiveradjudge the debtor bankrupt unless-

> *(a)* within 1 month of the date of the receiving order the debtor submits a proposal under section 20 which-
>
> > **(i)** in the opinion of the Official Receiver appears to be reasonable and calculated to benefit the general body of creditors; and

> **(ii)** is one which the court is not bound to refuse to approve; and
>
> *(b)* the court approves the composition.

(2) On the adjudication the property of the bankrupt shall become divisible among his creditors and shall vest in a trustee.

(3) The provisions of this section shall be in substitution for section 22(1).

Trustee

100D.(1) The court may on application being made by the Official Receiver by order appoint the Official Receiver or such other person recommended by him trustee of the property of the bankrupt, remove any trustee and fill any vacancy. Upon making any order for the appointment or removal of a trustee or for filling any vacancy the provisions of section 23(1) and (4), 81(1), (2) and (3) or 96(1), as the case may be, shall cease to apply to the bankruptcy and any action taken under such provisions in respect of any appointment or removal of a trustee or filling of any vacancy shall cease to have effect.

(2) The court may by order give such directions to a trustee as it shall think fit. Such directions shall be deemed to be the directions of creditors for the purposes of section 82. Neither a trustee nor the Official Receiver shall be required to summon any meetings of creditors save where the court so orders.

Committee of inspection

100E.(1) The court may on application being made by the Official Receiver or trustee by order appoint such qualified persons as it thinks fit as a committee of inspection for the purpose of superintending the administration of the property of the bankrupt by the trustee, remove any member thereof and fill any vacancy therein.

(2) The continuing members of the committee, provided there be not less than 2 such continuing members, may act notwithstanding any vacancy in their body.

(3) Upon the making of any order for such appointment, removal or filling of a vacancy the provisions of section 24(1), (7), (8) or (9), as the case may be, shall cease to apply to the bankruptcy and any action taken under such provisions in respect of any appointment of a committee of inspection, any removal of any member thereof or the filling of any vacancy therein shall cease to have effect.

Informing creditors and ascertaining their wishes

100F. The court may by order give such directions to the Official Receiver or trustee as it shall think fit for the purpose of keeping creditors informed of any matter relating to the bankruptcy and for ascertaining their wishes, and may require the Official Receiver or trustee to make such reports to the court as it may specify.

Creditors to give notice of intention to take part in public examination

100G.(1) The court may order that any creditor wishing to exercise his right to question the debtor on his public examination under section 19(4) shall give notice in writing of such intention to the Official Receiver, and may direct that no creditor may exercise such right unless notice is received by the Official Receiver within such time as may be specified.

(2) For the purpose of this section the court may direct that notice of the public examination of a debtor shall be published in such manner as it may specify, and notice of such examination or of adjourned hearings thereof shall not be required to be sent to creditors individually.

Proof of debts in the case of banks

100H.(1) Where the bankrupt was carrying on the business of a bank, any creditor who is a depositor, whether on current, savings, deposit, fixed deposit or other account, shall, unless and until the Official Receiver by notice in writing requires him to make a formal proof of debt, be deemed to have proved his debt-

> *(a)* for voting purposes, for the net balance to his credit in the books of the bank on all his accounts taken together, at the date of the receiving order:

Provided that if the said balance does not exceed $100 he shall not be deemed to have proved his debt for the purposes of sections 20(2) and (4), 25(1) and 100B(4); and

> *(b)* for dividend purposes, for the said balance plus or minus, as the case may be, the net amount of interest accrued due by or to the bank on the said accounts at the date of the receiving order.

(2) Any debt which is deemed to have been proved by virtue of subsection (1)shall be treated as if a proof thereof had been duly lodged in due time with the Official Receiver or trustee and had been admitted for voting and dividend purposes respectively for the said amounts stated in subsection (1).

Consolidation of petitions

101. Where 2 or more bankruptcy petitions are presented against the same debtor or against joint debtors the court may consolidate the proceedings or any of them on such terms as the court thinks fit.

Power to change carriage of proceedings

102. Where the petitioner does not proceed with due diligence on his petition the court may either dismiss the petition or substitute as petitioner any other creditor to whom the debtor may be indebted in the amount required by this Ordinance in the place of the petitioning creditor.

Continuance of proceedings on death of debtor

103. If a debtor by or against whom a bankruptcy petition has been presenteddies, the proceedings in the matter shall, unless the court otherwise orders, be continued as if he were alive.

Power to stay proceedings

104. The court may at any time, for sufficient reason, make an order staying theproceedings under a bankruptcy petition, either altogether or for a limited time, on such terms and subject to such conditions as the court may think just.

Power to present petition against one partner

105. Any creditors whose debt is sufficient to entitle him to present a bankruptcy petition against all the partners of a firm may present a petition against any one or more partners of the firm without including the others.

Power to dismiss petition against some respondents only

106. Where there are more respondents than one to a petition the court may dismiss the petition as to one or more of them without prejudice to the effect of the petition as against the other or others of them.

Actions by trustee and bankrupt's partners

107. Where a member of a partnership is adjudged bankrupt the court mayauthorize the trustee to commence and prosecute any action in the names of the trustee and of the bankrupt's partner; and any release by such partner of the debt or demand to which the action relates shall be void; but notice of the application for authority to commence the action shall be given to him, and he may show cause against it, and on his application the court may, if it thinks fit, direct that he shall receive his proper share of the proceeds of the action, and if he does not claim any benefit therefrom he shall be indemnified against costs in respect thereof as the court directs.

Actions on joint contracts

108. Where a bankrupt is a contractor in respect of any contract jointly withany person or persons, such person or persons may sue or be sued in respect ofthe contract without the joinder of the bankrupt.

Proceedings in partnership name

109. Any 2 or more persons, being partners, or any person carrying on businessunder a partnership name, may take proceedings or be proceeded against under this Ordinance in the name of the firm, but in such case the court may, on application by any person interested, order the names of the persons who are partners in such firm or the name of such person to be disclosed in such manner, and verified on oath or otherwise, as the court may direct.

PART VII - Supplemental Provisions

Disobedience to order of court
Disobedience to order of court

110. Where default is made by a trustee, debtor or other person in obeying any order or direction made or given by the court under this Ordinance, the court may make an immediate order for the committal of such trustee, debtor or other person for contempt of court: (*See Forms 98, 101*)

Provided that the power given by this section shall be deemed to be in addition to and not in substitution for any other right, remedy or liability in respect of such default.

Application of Ordinance
Exclusion of corporations, companies and limited partnerships

111. A receiving order shall not be made against any corporation, or against any association or company registered under the Companies Ordinance (Cap. 32), or any enactment repealed by that Ordinance, or against any partnership registered under the Limited Partnerships Ordinance (Cap. 37).

Administration in bankruptcy of estate of person dying insolvent

112.(1) Any creditor of a deceased debtor whose debt would have been sufficient to support a bankruptcy petition against the debtor, had he been alive, may present to the court a petition in the prescribed form praying for an order for the administration in bankruptcy of the estate of the deceased debtor, according to the law of bankruptcy. (*See Form 134*)

(2) The petition shall be served on the legal personal representative of the deceased debtor or, if there is none in Hong Kong, on the Official Administrator, and the court may in the prescribed manner, upon proof of the petitioner's debt, unless the court is satisfied that there is a reasonable probability that the estate will be sufficient for the payment of the debts owing by the deceased, make an order for the administration in bankruptcy of the deceased debtor's estate or may upon cause shown dismiss the petition with or without costs.

(3) A petition for administration in bankruptcy under this section shall not be presented to the court after proceedings have been commenced under the Rules of the Supreme Court (Cap. 4 sub. leg.) for the administration of the deceased debtor's estate but the court may, when satisfied that the estate is insufficient to pay its debts, make an order for the administration in bankruptcy of the estate of the deceased debtor and the like consequences shall ensue as under an administration order made on the petition of a creditor.

(4) Upon an order being made for the administration in bankruptcy of a deceased debtor's estate the property of the debtor shall vest in the Official Receiver as trustee thereof and he shall forthwith proceed to realize and distribute it in accordance with the provisions of this Ordinance: (*See Form 136*)

Provided that the creditors shall have the same powers as to appointment of trustees and committees of inspection as they have in other cases where the estate of a debtor is being administered or dealt with in bankruptcy, and the provisions of this Ordinance relating to trustees and committees of inspection shall apply to trustees and committees of inspection appointed under the power so conferred. If no committee of inspection is appointed any act or thing or any direction or permission which might have been done or given by a committee of inspection may be done or given by the court.

(5) With the modifications hereinafter mentioned, all the provisions of Part III (relating to the administration of the property of a bankrupt) and, subject to any modification that may be made therein by general rules under subsection (10) the following provisions, namely section 29 (which relates to inquiries as to the debtor's conduct, dealings and property) and section 86 (which relates to the costs of trustees, managers and other persons) shall, so far as the same are applicable, apply to the case of an administration order under this section in like manner as to an order of adjudication under this Ordinance, and section 40 shall apply as if for the reference to an order of adjudication there were substituted a reference to an administration order under this section.

(6) In the administration of the property of the deceased debtor under an order of administration the Official Receiver or trustee shall have regard to any claim by the legal personal representative of the deceased debtor to payment of the proper funeral and testamentary expenses incurred by him in and about the debtor's estate, and such claims shall be deemed a preferential debt under the order and shall, notwithstanding anything to the contrary in the provisions of this Ordinance relating to the priority of other debts, be payable in full out of the debtor's estate in priority to all other debts.

(7) If on the administration of a deceased debtor's estate any surplus remains in the hands of the Official Receiver or trustee, after payment in full of all the debts due from the debtor together with the costs of the administration and interest as provided by this Ordinance in case of bankruptcy, such surplus shall be paid over to the legal personal representative of the deceased debtor's estate, or failing such representative, to the Official Administrator.

(8) Service on the legal personal representative of a deceased debtor or on the Official Administrator of a petition under this section shall, in the event of an order for administration being made thereon, be deemed to be equivalent to notice of an act of bankruptcy, and after such service no payment or transfer of property made by the legal personal representative shall operate as a discharge to him as between himself and the Official Receiver or trustee; save as aforesaid nothing in this section shall invalidate any payment made or any act or thing done in good faith by the legal personal representative before the date of the order for administration.

(9) A petition for the administration of the estate of a deceased debtor under this section may be presented by the legal personal representative of the debtor or by the Official Administrator; and where a petition is so presented by such a representative or by the Official Administrator this section shall apply subject to such modifications as may be prescribed by general rules made under subsection (10). (*See Form 135*)

(10) General rules for carrying into effect the provisions of this section may be made in the same manner and to the like effect and extent as in bankruptcy.

Application of Ordinance to small bankruptcies

112A.(1) Subject to subsection (2), where a petition is presented by or against a debtor and-

    (a)   the court receives proof to its satisfaction; or

    (b)   the Official Receiver reports to the court,

that the property of the debtor is not likely to exceed in value $200,000, the court may make an order that the debtor's estate be administered in a summary manner, and thereupon the provisions of this Ordinance shall apply subject to the following modifications-

    (ia)   the Official Receiver may dispense with the summoning of the first meeting of creditors required under section 17, and instead apply to the court for an order adjudging the debtor bankrupt;

    (i)   if the debtor is adjudged bankrupt the Official Receiver shall be the trustee in the bankruptcy;

    (ii)   there shall be no committee of inspection, and the Official Receiver may do all things which may be done by a trustee with the permission of a committee of inspection;

    (iii)   such other modifications as may be prescribed with a view to saving expense and simplifying procedure, but nothing in this section shall permit the modification of the provisions of this Ordinance relating to the examination or discharge of the debtor.

(2) The court may, upon the application of the Official Receiver, at any time before the discharge of the debtor rescind an order made under subsection (1) and thereupon the administration shall proceed as if the order had not been made.

General rules

Power to make general rules

113. The Chief Justice may, with the approval of the Legislative Council, makerules providing for, generally, the carrying into effect the objects of this Ordinance.

Fees and remuneration

114.(1) The Chief Justice may, with the approval of the Legislative Council, by order prescribe a scale of fees and percentages to be charged for or in respect of proceedings under this Ordinance.

(2) The court may remit the payment of any particular fee or fees due from any debtor, or any part thereof, either absolutely or on such terms as it may think fit.

(3) The amount of any fees prescribed under this section shall not be limited by reference to the amount of administrative or other costs incurred or likely to be incurred by the Official Receiver in proceedings in bankruptcy or in any particular bankruptcy.

(4) Orders made under this section may authorize the court to fix any fee or to vary the amount of any fee otherwise prescribed.

(5) No fee prescribed under this section shall be invalid by reason only of the amount of that fee.

(6) Fees required to be paid under orders made under this section shall be recoverable as a debt.

(7) Orders made under this section before the commencement of the Bankruptcy (Amendment) Ordinance 1987 and in force immediately before such commencement, shall have effect as from the commencement of that Ordinance as if made under this section as amended by that Ordinance.

Disposal of Official Receiver's fees

115. All fees and commissions received by or payable to the Official Receiver on the appointment of a trustee other than himself or for acting as trustee, and any remuneration received by the Official Receiver as an interim receiver or otherwise, shall be paid by such officer forthwith into the general revenue.

Evidence

Evidence of proceedings at meetings of creditors

116.(1) A minute of proceedings at a meeting of creditors under this Ordinance, signed by a person describing himself as or appearing to be chairman of the meeting, shall be received in evidence without further proof.

(2) Until the contrary is proved every meeting of creditors in respect of the proceedings whereof a minute has been so signed shall be deemed to have been duly convened and held and all resolutions passed or proceedings had thereat to have been duly passed or had.

Evidence of proceedings in bankruptcy

117. Any petition or copy of a petition in bankruptcy, any order or certificateor copy of an order or certificate made by the court, any instrument or copy of an instrument, affidavit or document made or used in the course of any bankruptcy proceedings or other proceedings had under this Ordinance shall, if it appears to be sealed with the seal of the court or purports to be signed by the Registrar, or is certified as a true copy by the Registrar, be receivable in evidence in all legal proceedings whatsoever.

Swearing of affidavits

118. Subject to general rules, any affidavit to be used in a bankruptcy court may be sworn before any person authorized to administer oaths, or in the case of a person who is out of Hong Kong, before a magistrate or justice of the peace or other person qualified to administer oaths in the country where he resides (he being certified to be a magistrate or justice of the peace, or qualified as aforesaid, by a British minister or British consul or by a notary public).

Death of debtor or witness

119. In the case of the death of the debtor or his wife, or of a witness whose evidence has been received by the court in any proceeding under this Ordinance, the deposition of the person so deceased, purporting to be sealed with the seal of the court, or a copy thereof purporting to be so sealed, shall be admitted as evidence of the matters therein deposed to.

Statements made to Official Receiver or trustee through an interpreter

120. Any statement made by a debtor or creditor in any bankruptcy to the Official Receiver or trustee through an interpreter shall be deemed to have been made to the Official Receiver or trustee as the case may be respectively, and evidence thereof shall be receivable from the Official Receiver or trustee, on it being proved either that the interpreter employed was a sworn interpreter or that he held the substantive or acting appointment of interpreter, or of clerk and interpreter, to the Official Receiver.

Certificate of appointment of trustee

121. A certificate of the Official Receiver that a person has been appointed trustee under this Ordinance shall be conclusive evidence of his appointment.

Miscellaneous
Computation of time

122.(1) Where by this Ordinance any limited time from or after any date or event is appointed or allowed for the doing of any act or the taking of any proceeding, then in the computation of that limited time the same shall be taken as exclusive of the day of that date or of the happening of that event, and as commencing at the beginning of the next following day; and the act or proceeding shall be done or taken at latest on the last day of that limited time as so computed.

(2) Where the limited time so appointed or allowed is less than 6 days, general holidays as defined by the Holidays Ordinance (Cap. 149) shall not be reckoned in the computation of such time.

(3) Where the limited time so appointed or allowed expires on one of the days in this section specified, the act or proceeding shall be considered as done or taken in due time if it is done or taken on the next day afterwards which is not one of the days in this section specified.

(4) The provisions of this section shall take effect notwithstanding anything contained in sections 29, 30 and 31 of the Supreme Court Ordinance (Cap.4).

Service of notices

123. All notices and other documents for the service of which no special mode isdirected may be sent by post to the last known address of the person to be served therewith.

Formal defect not to invalidate proceedings

124.(1) No proceeding in bankruptcy shall be invalidated by any formal defect or by any irregularity unless the court is of opinion that substantial injustice has been caused by the defect or irregularity and that the injustice cannot be remedied by any order of the court.

(2) No defect or irregularity in the appointment or election of a receiver, trustee or member of a committee of inspection shall vitiate any act done by him in good faith.

Exemption of documents from stamp duty

125.(1) Stamp duty shall not be payable in respect of-

(a) any assurance relating solely to immovable property or personal property which is part of the estate of any bankrupt, and which, after the execution of the assurance, either at law or in equity, is or remains the estate of the bankrupt or of the trustee under the bankruptcy; or

(b) any other instrument relating solely to the property of any bankrupt.

(2) In this section "assurance" includes deed, conveyance, assignment and surrender.

Acting of corporations, partners, etc.

126. For all or any of the purposes of this Ordinance a corporation may act by any of its officers authorized in that behalf under the seal of the corporation, a firm may act by any of its members and a lunatic may act by his committee or curator bonis.

Certain provisions to bind Crown

127. Save as provided in this Ordinance, the provisions of this Ordinance relating to the remedies against the property of a debtor, the priorities of debts, the effect of a composition or scheme of arrangement, and the effect of a discharge, shall bind the Crown.

Unclaimed funds or dividends
Unclaimed and undistributed dividends or funds

128.(1) Where a trustee, other than the Official Receiver, under any bankruptcy, composition or scheme, pursuant to this Ordinance has under his control any unclaimed dividend which has remained unclaimed for more than 6 months, or any money held in trust by the debtor for another person, or where, after making a final dividend, he has in his hands or under his control any unclaimed or undistributed money arising from the property of the debtor, he shall forthwith pay it to the Official Receiver who shall carry the same to an account to be termed the Bankruptcy Estate Account. The Official Receiver's receipt for the money so paid shall be a sufficient discharge to the trustee in respect thereof.

(1A) Where the Official Receiver is the trustee, and under any bankruptcy, composition or scheme, pursuant to this Ordinance has under his control any unclaimed dividend which has remained unclaimed for more than 6 months or where after making a final dividend, he has in his hands or under his control any unclaimed or undistributed money arising from the property of the debtor, he shall forthwith transfer the same to the Bankruptcy Estates Account.

(2) The trustee, whether he has obtained his release or not, may be called upon by the court to account for any unclaimed funds or dividends and any failure to comply with the requisitions of the court in this behalf may be dealt with as a contempt of court.

(3) Any person claiming to be entitled to any moneys paid into the Bankruptcy Estate Account under this Ordinance may, within 5 years of the date when the same was so paid in, apply to the Official Receiver for payment to him of the same, and the Official Receiver, if satisfied that the person claiming is entitled, shall make an order for the payment to such person of the sum due. Any person dissatisfied with the decision of the Official Receiver may appeal to the court.

(4) After any money has remained unclaimed in the Bankruptcy Estates Account for a period of 5 years the Official Receiver may transfer such money to the general revenue of Hong Kong.

(5) Before transferring any money under subsection (4) the Official Receiver may give such notice as he thinks necessary to such parties as he may think fit.

Deposit of surplus cash balances

128A.(1) Whenever the cash balance standing to the credit of-

      (a) the Bankruptcy Estates Account referred to in section 128; or

(b)   any account operated by the Official Receiver under section 91,

is in excess of the amount which, in the opinion of the Official Receiver, is required for the time being to answer demands in respect of debtor's estates, the Official Receiver may deposit the whole or any part of that excess with a bank.

(2)   The Official Receiver shall on or after 31 March in each year transfer to the general revenue any interest paid in respect of deposits under subsection (1).

PART VIII - Bankruptcy Offences

Fraudulent debtors

129.(1) Any person who has been adjudged bankrupt or in respect of whose estate a receiving order has been made shall in each of the cases following be guilty of an offence-

(a)   if he does not to the best of his knowledge and belief fully and truly discover to the trustee all his property, real and personal, and how and to whom and for what consideration and when he disposed of any part thereof, except such part as has been disposed of in the ordinary way of his trade (if any) or laid out in the ordinary expenses of his family, unless he proves that he had no intent to defraud;

(b)   if he does not deliver up to the trustee, or as he directs, all such part of his movable or immovable property as is in his custody or under his control and which he is required by law to deliver up, unless he proves that he had no intent to defraud;

(c)   if he does not deliver up to the trustee, or as he directs, all books, documents, papers and writings in his custody or under his control relating to his property or affairs, unless he proves that he had no intent to defraud;

(d)   if, after the presentation of a bankruptcy petition by or against him or within 12 months next before such presentation, he conceals any part of his property to the value of $50 or upwards or conceals any debt due to or from him, unless he proves that he had no intent to defraud;

(e)   if, after the presentation of a bankruptcy petition by or against him or within 12 months next before such presentation, he fraudulently removes any part of his property to the value of $50 or upwards;

(f)   if he makes any material omission or misstatement in any statement relating to his affairs, unless he proves that he had no intent to defraud;

(g)   if, knowing or having any reason to believe that a false debt has been proved by any person under the bankruptcy, he fails for the period of a month to inform the trustee thereof;

(h)   if, after the presentation of a bankruptcy petition by or against him, he prevents or is party or privy to preventing the production of any book, document, paper or writing affecting or relating to his property or affairs, unless he proves that he had no intent to conceal the state of his affairs or to defeat the law;

(i)   if, after the presentation of a bankruptcy petition by or against him or within 12 months next before such presentation, he removes, conceals, destroys, mutilates or falsifies or is privy to the removal, concealment, destruction, mutilation or falsification of any book or document affecting or relating to his property or affairs, unless he proves that he had no intent to conceal the state of his affairs or to defeat the law;

(j)   if, after the presentation of a bankruptcy petition by or against him or within 12 months next before such presentation, he makes or is privy to the making of any false entry in any book or document affecting or relating to his property or affairs, unless he proves that he had no intent to conceal the state of his affairs or to defeat the law;

(k)   if, after the presentation of a bankruptcy petition by or against him or within 12 months next before such presentation, he fraudulently parts with, alters or makes any omission in, or is privy to the fraudulently parting with, altering or making any omission in, any document affecting or relating to his property or affairs;

(l)   if, after the presentation of a bankruptcy petition by or against him or at any meeting of his creditors within 12 months next before such presentation, he attempts to account for any part of his property by fictitious losses or expenses;

(m)-(n) *(Repealed)*

(o)   if, within 12 months next before the presentation of a bankruptcy petition by or against him or after the presentation of a bankruptcy petition and before the making of a receiving order, he pawns, pledges or disposes of any property which he has obtained on credit and has not paid for, unless, in the case of a trader, such pawning, pledging or disposing is in the ordinary way of his trade, and unless in any case he proves that he had no intent to defraud;

    (p)   if he is guilty of any false representation or other fraud for the purpose of obtaining the consent of his creditors or any of them to an agreement with reference to his affairs or to his bankruptcy.

(2) A person who has sent out of Hong Kong any property which he has obtained on credit and has not paid for shall until the contrary is proved be deemed to have disposed of the same otherwise than in the ordinary way of his trade if, such property not having been paid or accounted for at the date of the receiving order by the person to whom the same was sent, such last-mentioned person does not pay or account for the same within a reasonable time after being called upon to do so by the trustee or cannot be found within a reasonable time.

(3) In any prosecution under subsection (1)(i) the absence of any such book or document as is referred to in the said paragraph shall be prima facie evidence that such book or document was removed by the debtor contrary to the provisions of the said paragraph or that he was privy to its removal contrary to those provisions, and thereupon the onus shall be upon the debtor to prove that he did not so remove such book or document and that he was not privy to such removal.

(4) In any prosecution under subsection (1)(i) the mutilation or falsification of any such book or document as is referred to in the said paragraph shall be prima facie evidence that such book or document was mutilated or falsified by the debtor in contravention of the provisions of the said paragraph or that he was privy to its mutilation or falsification contrary to those provisions, and thereupon the onus shall be upon the debtor to prove that he did not so mutilate or falsify the said book or document and that he was not privy to such mutilation or falsification.

(5) Any person guilty of an offence in the cases mentioned in subsection (1)(o) shall be liable on summary conviction to imprisonment for 1 year or upon conviction on indictment to imprisonment for 5 years.

(6) For the purposes of this section, "trustee" includes the Official Receiver, whether acting as Official Receiver or as a trustee.

Certain offences by persons other than the debtor

130.(1) If any manager, accountant or book-keeper in the employment of the debtor does any act which if committed by the debtor would be a contravention of any of the provisions of section 129(1)(i) or (j), or is privy to any such act whether committed by the debtor or by any other person, such manager, accountant or book-keeper shall be deemed to be guilty of an offence.

(2) Where any person pawns, pledges or disposes of any property in circumstances which amount to an offence under section 129(1)(o), every person who takes in pawn or pledge or otherwise receives the property, knowing it to be pawned, pledged or disposed of in such circumstances as aforesaid, shall be guilty of an offence and shall be liable on summary conviction to imprisonment for 1 year or upon conviction on indictment to imprisonment for 5 years.

Undischarged bankrupt obtaining credit

131.   Any undischarged bankrupt shall in each of the cases following be guilty of an offence-

(a)   if either alone or jointly with any other person he obtains credit to the extent of $100 or upwards from any person without first informing that person that he is an undischarged bankrupt; or

(b)   if he engages in any trade or business under a name or names other than that or those under which he was adjudicated bankrupt and in the course of such trade or business obtains credit from any person without first disclosing to such person the name or names under which he was adjudicated bankrupt; or

(c)   if he engages in any trade or business under a name or names other than that or those under which he was adjudicated bankrupt without first publishing, once in the Gazette, and in 3 successive issues of 2 local newspapers one of which shall be Chinese, a notice containing the following particulars-

(i)   the name or names under which he was adjudicated bankrupt;

(ii)   the last address at which he carried on any trade or business prior to the adjudication;

(iii)   the name or names under which he intends to carry on the trade or business;

(iv)   the nature of the trade or business which he intends to carry on; and

(v)   the address or addresses at which he intends to carry it on.

Frauds by bankrupts, etc.

132. Any person who has been adjudged bankrupt or in respect of whose estate a receiving order has been made shall in each of the cases following be guilty of an offence-

(a)   *(Repealed)*

(b)   if with intent to defraud his creditors or any of them he has made or caused to be made any gift or transfer of or charge on his property; or

(c)   if with intent to defraud his creditors he had concealed or removed any part of his property since or within 2 months before the date of any unsatisfied judgment or order for payment of money obtained against him; or

(d)   if with intent to defraud his creditors or any of them he has caused or connived at the levying of any execution against his property.

Bankrupt guilty of gambling, etc.

133.(1) Any person who has been adjudged bankrupt, or in respect of whose estate a receiving order has been made, shall be guilty of an offence if, having been engaged in any trade or business and having outstanding at the date of the receiving order any debts contracted in the course and for the purposes of such trade or business-

(a)   he has within 2 years prior to the presentation of the bankruptcy petition materially contributed to or increased the extent of his insolvency by gambling or by rash and hazardous speculations and such gambling or speculations are unconnected with his trade or business; or

(b)   he has between the date of the presentation of the petition and the date of the receiving order lost any part of his estate by such gambling or rash and hazardous speculations as aforesaid; or

(c)   on being required by the Official Receiver at any time, or in the course of his public examination by the court, to account for the loss of any substantial part of his estate incurred within a period of a year next preceding the date of the presentation of the bankruptcy petition or between that date and the date of the receiving order, he fails to give a satisfactory explanation of the manner in which such loss was incurred:

Provided that, in determining for the purposes of this section whether any speculations were rash and hazardous, the financial position of the accused person at the time when he entered into the speculations shall be taken into consideration.

(2) A prosecution shall not be instituted against any person under this section except by order of the court.

Bankrupt failing to keep proper accounts

134.(1) Any person who has been adjudged bankrupt or in respect of whose estate a receiving order has been made shall be guilty of an offence if, having been engaged in any trade or business during any period in the 2 years immediately preceding the date of the presentation of the bankruptcy petition, he has not kept proper books of account throughout that period and throughout any further period in which he was so engaged between the date of the presentation of the petition and the date of the receiving order, or has not preserved all books of account so kept:

Provided that a person who has not kept or has not preserved such books of account shall not be convicted of an offence under this section-

      (a)   if his unsecured liabilities at the date of the receiving order did not exceed, in the case of a person who has not on any previous occasion in Hong Kong or elsewhere been adjudged bankrupt or made a composition or arrangement with his creditors, $5,000 or in any other case $1,000; or

      (b)   if he proves that in the circumstances in which he traded or carried on business the omission was honest and excusable.

(2) A prosecution shall not be instituted against any person under this section except by order of the court.

(3) For the purposes of this section, a person shall be deemed not to have kept proper books of account if he has not kept such books or accounts as are necessary to exhibit or explain his transactions and financial position in his trade or business, including a book or books containing entries from day to day in sufficient detail of all cash received and cash paid, and where the trade or business has involved dealings in goods, statements of annual stock-takings, and (except in the case of goods sold by way of retail trade to the actual consumer) accounts of all goods sold and purchased showing the buyers and sellers thereof in sufficient detail to enable the goods and the buyers and sellers thereof to be identified. In the case of books or accounts kept in the Chinese language a person shall, for the purposes of this section, be deemed not to have kept proper books of account if he has not kept such books or accounts as may be proved to be usual and necessary, for the purposes aforesaid, in the particular trade or business carried on by the debtor.

Bankrupt absconding with property

135. If any person who is adjudged bankrupt, or in respect of whose estate a receiving order has been made, after the presentation of a bankruptcy petition by or against him, or within 6 months before such presentation, quits Hong Kong and takes with him, or attempts or makes preparation to quit Hong Kong and take with him, any part of his property to the amount of $100 or upwards, which ought by law to be divided amongst his creditors, he shall (unless he proves that he had no intent to defraud) be guilty of an offence.

Debtor concealing himself to avoid service, etc.

136. If any person against whom a receiving order is made conceals himself or absents himself from his usual or last known place of abode or business or quits Hong Kong, with intent to avoid service of any process in bankruptcy or to avoid examination in respect of his affairs or otherwise to defeat, embarrass or delay any proceedings against him in bankruptcy, he shall be guilty of an offence. A person who, after the presentation of a bankruptcy petition by or against him or within 3 months next before such presentation, conceals or absents himself as aforesaid or quits Hong Kong shall until the contrary is proved be deemed to have concealed or absented himself or quitted Hong Kong with such intent as is mentioned in this section.

137. (*Repealed*)

Order by court for prosecution on report of trustee

138. Where the Official Receiver or a trustee in a bankruptcy reports to the court that in his opinion a debtor who has been adjudged bankrupt or in respect of whose estate a receiving order has been made has been guilty of any offence under this Ordinance, or where the court is satisfied upon the representation of any creditor or member of the committee of inspection that there is ground to believe that the debtor has been guilty of any such offence, the court shall, if it appears to the court that there is a reasonable probability that the debtor will be convicted and that the circumstances are such as to render a prosecution desirable, order that the debtor be prosecuted for such offence, but no such order shall be a condition antecedent to any prosecution under this Ordinance.

Criminal liability after discharge or composition

139. Where a debtor has been guilty of any criminal offence he shall not be exempt from being proceeded against therefor by reason that he has obtained his discharge or that a composition or scheme of arrangement has been accepted or approved.

Trial and punishment of offenses

140.(1) A person guilty of an offence under this Ordinance in respect of which no special penalty is imposed by this Ordinance shall be guilty of an offence triable either summarily or upon indictment, and shall be liable to imprisonment for 2 years.

(2) Summary proceedings in respect of any such offence shall not be instituted after 1 year from the first discovery thereof either by the Official Receiver or by the trustee in the bankruptcy, or in the case of proceedings instituted by a creditor, by the creditor, nor in any case shall they be instituted after 3 years from the commission of the offence.

(3) In an indictment for an offence under this Ordinance it shall be sufficient to set forth the substance of the offence charged in the words of this Ordinance specifying the offence, or as near thereto as circumstances admit, without alleging or setting forth any debt, act of bankruptcy, trading, adjudication, or any proceedings in, or order, warrant or document of, the court acting under this Ordinance.

Evidence as to frauds by agents

141. A statement or admission made by any person in any compulsory examination or deposition before the court on the hearing of any matter in bankruptcy shall not be admissible as evidence against that person or (unless they married after the making of the statement or admission) against the wife or husband of that person in any proceeding in respect of an offence under the Theft Ordinance (Cap. 210).

Summaryprosecution

142. Any offence under this Ordinance may be dealt with summarily by a magistrate.

PART IX - Miscellaneous

143. (*Omitted as spent*)

SCHEDULE 1

Criminal Bankruptcy Orders

PART I - General

Interpretation

1. In this Schedule-

"criminal bankruptcy debt" means a debt deemed to be due to any person by virtue of paragraph 3.

Act of bankruptcy

2. Subject to the provisions of this Schedule, where a criminal bankruptcy order is made against any person he shall be treated as a debtor who has committed an act of bankruptcy on the date on which the order is made.

Creditors and criminal bankruptcy debts

3. A person specified in a criminal bankruptcy order as having suffered loss or damage of any amount shall be treated for the purpose of any ensuing proceedings pursuant to-

(a)   a bankruptcy petition presented by virtue of paragraph 2; or

(b)   a petition under section 112 (administration in bankruptcy of estate of person dying insolvent) presented by virtue of this Schedule,

as a creditor for a debt of that amount provable in the bankruptcy of the person against whom the order was made.

PART II - Application Of The Ordinance In Proceedings Based On A

Criminal Bankruptcy Order

Criminal bankruptcy petition

4. No criminal bankruptcy petition shall be presented by the person who under paragraph 2 is the debtor; and, in relation to such a petition presented by a creditor, section 6 shall have effect with the following modifications-

> *(a)* subsections (1)(a) and (b) and (2) (conditions as to nature of debt) shall not apply to a criminal bankruptcy debt; and

> *(b)* subsection (1)(d) (domicile of debtor) shall be omitted.

Receiving order

5. For the purposes of section 9(2) and (3) (matters to be proved before receiving order is made) the act of bankruptcy which a person is treated by this Schedule as having committed and any criminal bankruptcy debt shall be treated as conclusively proved by the production of a copy of the criminal bankruptcy order in question and the following provisions of that section shall not apply in relation to any such debt-

> *(a)* so much of subsection (3) which provides that if the court is not satisfied that the assets for division among the unsecured creditors, after payment of all costs, charges and expenses, and the debts which are preferential under that Ordinance, will be sufficient to pay a dividend of 15 per cent, it may dismiss the petition;

> *(b)* subsection (5);

> *(c)* subsection (6).

Trustee of criminal bankrupt's property

6. Where a person is adjudged bankrupt in proceedings pursuant to a criminal bankruptcy petition the Official Receiver shall in the bankruptcy be the trustee of the property of the bankrupt and section 23 shall not apply in relation to any such proceedings.

Proof of criminal bankruptcy debt in bankruptcy proceedings

7.(1) For the purpose of proving a criminal bankruptcy debt in proceedings pursuant to a criminal bankruptcy petition, a copy of the criminal bankruptcy order specifying the amount deemed by virtue of paragraph 3 to be due as a debt shall, subject to paragraph 5, be treated as sufficient evidence of the debt unless it is shown by any party to the proceedings that the amount of the relevant loss or damage is greater or less than the amount specified in the order or that the loss or damage did not in fact result from any offence specified in the order; and if it is shown by any party to the proceedings that the amount of the relevant loss or damage is other than that specified in the order, paragraph 3 shall have effect as if that other amount had been specified in the order, but without prejudice to the validity of the order if the amount of the relevant loss is shown not to exceed $150,000 or such other amount as may be specified in an order made under section 84A(5) of the Criminal Procedure Ordinance (Cap. 221).

(2) Nothing in this paragraph or paragraph 3 shall be taken as prejudicing the proof in proceedings pursuant to a criminal bankruptcy petition of debts other than criminal bankruptcy debts.

(3) Nothing in sub-paragraph (1) shall be construed as entitling any person to contend that the offence or offences specified in a criminal bankruptcy order were not committed by the person against whom the order was made.

Recovery of assets for benefit of criminal bankrupt's creditors

8.(1) Without prejudice to any other provision of this Ordinance, sub-paragraph (2) to (5) shall apply, where a person is adjudged bankrupt in proceedings pursuant to a criminal bankruptcy petition, with respect to dispositions of property or any interest in property made by the bankrupt on or after the relevant date, either by way of gift or for an under-value.

In this sub-paragraph, "relevant date" means the date specified in the criminal bankruptcy order (in accordance with section 84A(3)(d) of the Criminal Procedure Ordinance (Cap. 221)) as the earliest date on which the offence or, as the case may be, the earliest of the offences, was committed.

(2) On the application of the Official Receiver (in his capacity as trustee) the court may make orders requiring-

> *(a)* the person taking under any such disposition; or

> *(b)* subject to sub-paragraph (3), any other person who by virtue of any subsequent disposition acquired (whether or not from the person taking under the bankrupt's disposition) the whole or any part of the property or any interest therein,

to transfer the whole or any part of the property, or such interest as the order may specify, to the trustee, or to make such payments to the trustee as the court thinks just with a view to making available to the creditors the full value of the property or interest disposed of by the bankrupt (including any increase in its value since the disposition was made).

(3) No order shall be made by virtue of sub-paragraph (2)(b) against a person appearing to the court to have given full value for anything taken by him under a relevant disposition or to claim (directly or indirectly) through a person who gave full value.

(4) An order of the court under this paragraph requiring a person to transfer any property or interest may include such consequential directions for giving effect to the order, and be made on such terms (including in particular terms allowing the person to retain or recover consideration given by him for any relevant disposition) as the court thinks just in all the circumstances.

(5) In this paragraph, "disposition" includes any conveyance or assurance of property of any description.

Administration in bankruptcy of deceased offender's estate

9.(1) Where an order for administration is made under section 112 on a criminal bankruptcy administration petition, so much of subsection (4) of that section as enables the creditors to appoint a trustee of the property of the debtor in place of the Official Receiver shall not apply.

(2) Paragraph 7 shall apply in relation to proof of criminal bankruptcy debts in proceedings pursuant to a criminal bankruptcy administration petition as it applies in relation to proof of such debts in proceedings pursuant to a criminal bankruptcy petition.

Bankruptcy proceedings otherwise than by virtue of this Schedule

10. Where a criminal bankruptcy order has been made against any person and a bankruptcy petition has been presented in respect of him before the order was made, or is presented in respect of him thereafter otherwise than by virtue of paragraph 2, the court may, on the application of the Official Petitioner, dismiss the petition, rescind any receiving order made in pursuance thereof or, if that person has been adjudged bankrupt, annul the adjudication on such terms, if any, as the court thinks fit.

Effect of appeal against conviction

11.(1) Subject to the provisions of this paragraph, the fact that an appeal is pending against any conviction by virtue of which a criminal bankruptcy order was made shall not preclude the taking of any proceedings by virtue of this Schedule in consequence of the making of the order.

(2) Where a person is adjudged bankrupt in proceedings pursuant to a criminal bankruptcy petition, no property shall be distributed by his trustee in bankruptcy and no order shall be made by the court under paragraph 8 so long as an appeal is pending against his conviction of any offence by virtue of which the criminal bankruptcy order was made.

(3) For the purposes of this paragraph an appeal against a conviction is pending-

> *(a)*   in any case until the expiration of the time for giving notice of appeal or applying for leave to appeal under section 83Q of the Criminal Procedure Ordinance (Cap. 221) (disregarding any extension of time which may be granted under subsection (3) of that section);

(b) if notice of appeal or of application for leave is given during that period and during that period the appellant notifies the Official Receiver thereof, until the determination of the appeal and thereafter for so long as an appeal to the Privy Council is pending within the meaning of section 84B(5) of that Ordinance.

(4) Where in consequence of an appeal a criminal bankruptcy order is rescinded-

(a) any bankruptcy petition based on the order shall lapse and any receiving order or adjudication of bankruptcy made in consequence thereof shall cease to have effect, but without prejudice to anything previously done thereunder;

(b) where any such adjudication ceases to have effect, the property of the person who was adjudicated bankrupt shall revert to him for all his estate or interest therein; and

(c) the court may, on his application or on the application of the Official Receiver, by order give such directions, if any, as appear to the said court to be necessary or desirable in consequence of the provisions of sub-paragraphs (a) and (b).

(5) Where in consequence of an appeal a criminal bankruptcy order is amended by the deletion of any amount specified therein as the loss or damage suffered by any person, paragraph 3 shall not thereafter apply to that loss or damage but without prejudice to anything done before the amendment takes effect.

PART III - Functions Of Official Petitioner

Presentation of criminal bankruptcy petition by Official Petitioner

12.(1) The Official Petitioner may present a criminal bankruptcy petition, and a receiving order may be made on that petition.

(2) Section 6, as modified by paragraph 4 of this Schedule, shall apply to a criminal bankruptcy petition presented by the Official Petitioner as it applies to a

petition presented by a creditor, but the court may allow the petition to be presented later than required by subsection (1)(c) of that section.

(3) The following provisions-

> (a)   section 9(2) (making of receiving order on creditor's petition);
>
> (b)   section 9(3) (dismissal of petition); and
>
> (c)   section 9(7) (withdrawal of creditor's petition),

shall apply in relation to a criminal bankruptcy petition presented by the Official Petitioner as if any reference to the debt of the petitioning creditor were a reference to any criminal bankruptcy debt within the meaning of this Schedule; and paragraph 5 shall have effect in relation to section 9(2) and (3) as they apply by virtue of this paragraph.

Presentation of criminal bankruptcy administration

petition by Official Petitioner

13.(1) The Official Petitioner may present a petition under section 112 in any case in which a creditor could do so by virtue of this Schedule, and an order may be made under that section on that petition.

(2) Section 112(2) shall have effect in relation to a petition presented by the Official Petitioner as if the reference to the petitioner's debt were a reference to any criminal bankruptcy debt within the meaning of this Schedule.

Participation of Official Petitioner in proceedings brought by virtue of this

Schedule (whether by the Official Petitioner or by a creditor)

14.(1) In the case of proceedings pursuant to a criminal bankruptcy petition or a criminal bankruptcy administration petition, the Official Petitioner shall be entitled-

> (a)   to attend any meeting of creditors and, before the meeting, to receive any notice or other document required to be sent before such a meeting to any creditor;
>
> (b)   to be a member of any committee of inspection appointed under section 24, but not so as to count towards the number of members mentioned in subsection (2) or (9), or be subject to removal under subsection (7), of that section;
>
> (c)   to be a party to any such proceedings before the court.

(2) In the case of proceedings pursuant to-

> (a)   a criminal bankruptcy petition or a criminal bankruptcy

administration petition, the provisions of the Ordinance mentioned in sub-paragraph (3) shall have effect as if any reference to a creditor, or to a creditor who has proved or tendered a proof, included a reference to the Official Petitioner; and

(b)   a criminal bankruptcy administration petition, the expression "a petition under this section" in section 112 (8) shall include a reference to a petition by the Official Petitioner.

(3) The provisions referred to in sub-paragraph (2) are-

(a)   section 15 (power to appoint special manager);

(b)   section 18(2) and (4) (debtor's statement of affairs);

(c)   section 19(4) and (8) (public examination of debtor);

(d)   section 20(5), (6) and (8) (compositions and schemes of arrangement);

(e)   section 30(2) and (8) (discharge of bankrupt);

(f)   section 42 (relation back of trustee's title);

(g)   section 78(1)(e) (report to creditors of debtor's proposal);

(h)   section 83 (appeal to court against act or decision of trustee).

SCHEDULE 2

[ss. 75 & 76]

Assistant Official Receiver (Legal)
Assistant Principal Solicitor
Senior Solicitor
Solicitor

PART II

Assistant Director of Accounting Services
Chief Insolvency Officer
Senior Insolvency Officer
Insolvency Officer
Senior Treasury Accountant
Treasury Accountant
Accounting Officer I
Accounting Officer II
Assistant Official Receiver (Case Management)

Hong Kong as a Tax Haven for International Business

by

Adam Starchild

Tax havens are very much in the news, and stories about small- and medium-sized companies mushrooming overnight and multi-national giants amassing fabulous fortunes via tax haven operations are growing. They may sound like Alice in Wonderland fairy tales to most people, but to the sophisticated entrepreneur, use of foreign tax havens for such advantages is an everyday business opportunity.

The use of a foreign corporation domiciled in any one of the famous company tax havens such as Hong Kong, Panama, the Bahamas, or Bermuda (among others, can enhance the profitability of any international business.

Many European and American companies are expanding and diversifying overseas as a means of growth and as a hedge against economic ups and downs in their country of origin. By incorporating a tax haven operation to accumulate tax-free income, accomplishment of multi-national objectives is accelerated. An international trading or freight operation can be established in a tax haven to be used as a conduit for international sales activity and financing. Such operations can accumulate trade discounts, commissions, advertising allowances, etc., completely tax-free while the parent or associated company can assume tax deductions by absorbing administrative and selling costs.

Before getting into the ways in which tax haven operations are used by various types of businesses, it is of eminent importance that the distinct difference is understood between two seemingly similar terms: "tax avoidance" and "tax evasion." Tax evasion has dubious and illegal overtones: for example, a company might falsify its financial statements so as to conceal its full liability to the tax authorities — that would be tax evasion — an infraction of the law and a very serious one.

Tax avoidance, on the other hand, is a legitimate method of minimizing or negating the tax factor. In simple terms, it is utilizing "loopholes" in tax laws and exploiting them within legal perimeters. This is the cornerstone of the tax haven concept.

Certain offshore companies can defer any tax until the profits are repatriated to the investor's home country. These are generally companies actively engaged in the conduct of a local business. In most import-export or other international trade activities, such a definition is especially easy to meet. A retailer, or group of retailers, could set up their own wholesale buying opertion in a convenient tax haven, such as Hong Kong, and put all of their Asian business through it. The profits of the Hong Kong firm would accumulate tax-free, and could be invested in other foreign operations.

In addition, a great many countries offer tax holidays of 5 to 20 years for new export manufacturers or assembly operations, often including smaller companies down to as few as ten employees. A company or group of companies could easily invest some of their foreign profits in such a venture, continuing to build for tax-free profits. Such concessions often include an exemption from customs duties on raw materials and equipment.

Most developed countries do tax the current income of certain types of corporations controlled by their residents, such as leasing companies, and other financial enterprises dealing the parent company. But this concept of a controlled foreign corporation applies usually to passive or tax-haven type corporations, not to active businesses. But even for a passive business, a joint venture with foreign partners on a 50-50 basis will allow the income to accumulate tax-free since the company is not controlled by national of either country. If you are leasing equipment, consider a joint venture with your foreign partner whereby you set up a jointly owned company to receive some of the income. You will both profit by it, and have a tax-free pool of funds to invest together in other ventures. Such profits will not be taxed in the country of either partner until they are repatriated, since they are not controlled by either country's citizen.

Countries which have no income tax include Bermuda, the Bahamas, the Cayman Islands, Nevis, and the Turks & Caicos Islands. A number of countries do not tax foreign source income, including Panama and Hong Kong.

Many businessmen looking for tax haven opportunities would envy the daily opportunities open to international traders, and yet most international traders rarely use these opportunities — or even understand them. 100% tax-free dollars will grow a whole lot faster than 50% after-tax dollars.

Setting Up Your Tax Haven-Based Trading Operation

A firm I can personally give my highest recommendation to is ICS Trust (Asia) Limited, based in Hong Kong.

The handover of the former British Crown Colony of Hong Kong to China is complete, and it is now called the Hong Kong Special Administrative Region, generally abbreviated to Hong Kong S.A.R., even on official documents.

As more than one local businessman has put it, "now that the politicians and journalists are gone (from covering the handover), we can get down to *business*." This attitude is typical of Hong Kong, still a true capitalist center. In fact, many of the wealthy who left to obtain second citizenships in Canada, Australia, and elsewhere, have now returned home to continue building their fortunes.

The major advantage of Hong Kong is simply that it is a real business center, not just a tax haven. One of the consequences of that is the ability to add value to services that are provided in only skeleton form in other tax havens. The reinvoicing business is a prime example. Most tax haven jurisdictions host a number of trading companies that do nothing more than reinvoicing. But one Hong Kong firm has now developed this traditional service into a "real" business mode, with an ability to arrange local trade financing. This is a healthy step away from traditional tax havenry into a true offshore **business** center.

ICS Trust Company Limited is part of the ICS International group of companies headquartered in Hong Kong. This highly successful entrepreneurial group was started by Elizabeth L. Thomson. Elizabeth describes herself as "a lawyer by profession" (2 law degrees, a member of 4 Law Societies internationally), "an entrepreneur by choice"! She has helped innumerable people start new enterprises in many parts of the globe and is well known in Hong Kong for her work with women entrepreneurs.

With a staff of 40 at ICS, every aspect of your business is covered — from deciding to incorporate, to obtaining financing from the bank, to managing your paper work including Letters of Credit, to investing your hard earned profits! ICS is truly a "one stop shop" for entrepreneurs.

Their clients range from multinational companies for whom they run Direct Import Programs worth millions of dollars to individuals who seek tax sheltering and estate planning on an international scale. As an entrepreneurial group, they attract many entrepreneurs as clients — business people who have grown their business to a level of maturity and profits that requires expansion into Asia for many diverse reasons.

Instead of just a paper thin traditional tax haven reinvoicing company, with ICS you can develop a real business in Hong Kong. With their extensive banking contacts, ICS professionals will "shop" for the best letter of credit facilities that Hong Kong's competitive banking scene can offer, likely better facilities than you can find at home. Depending upon the client, ICS can often arrange letter of credit banking facilities for clients with either a low or zero margin deposit, usually required by the opening bank. By freeing up your collateral and capital, they provide you with more purchasing power to increase sales and gain higher profits.

Most of these reinvoicing transactions are usually effected such that they are tax free in Hong Kong. There is no withholding tax on dividends so it is often possible to engage in international trade through a HK company and obtain dividends from that company tax free.

ICS will also work with international banks and factors in Hong Kong and overseas to arrange financing, secured primarily on the strength of purchase orders from your clients. Working with banks, factories, shipping companies and freight forwarders, ICS will structure a transaction to increase the likelihood of obtaining flexible, low cost facilities.

The goods do not need to go through HK for us to use a HK vehicle to pass title. Most of their clients ship from a third country direct to their own country.

Although the traditional Hong Kong focus is on firms who trade in goods, it is also possible to use these structures in cases where services are to be provided from overseas. For example, a firm could contract out a study to a company in Hong Kong. This Hong Kong company could then sub-contract out the work to a third party firm and the profit kept in Hong Kong, tax free.

If you import goods from Asia for sale to large chains, ICS can help you expand your credit facilities and increase your domestic sales by establishing and running a Direct Import Program for you. Combined with their international trade finance capabilities, the Direct Import Program is a powerful tool for generating more profits.

The primary goal of the Direct Import Program is to maximize your profits by making your customers perceive that they are buying "direct." This is achieved by:

- setting up a subsidiary company in Hong Kong

- getting your buyers to open their L/C or orders to this subsidiary

- liaising with suppliers to ensure goods are to specification.

The Direct Import Program works because of two powerful reasons:

- The trend in the retail industry is for buyers to "buy direct" from the Orient. Having a subsidiary in Hong Kong which receives orders or L/Cs greatly enhances this perception.

- Large retail chains often can obtain freight and insurance at significant savings because of their economies of scale. Selling FOB Asia can often result in a lower selling price for the importer but with the same profit.

ICS will set up and manage the subsidiary company for you, and prepare financing proposals for presentation to local banks. When everything is complete, goods are shipped directly from the Asian factory to the customer. The fact that you are now seen as an Asian supplier (and not the middleman) is often an important factor that clinches the deal. The added prestige of a Hong Kong office makes the customer think he or she is buying "direct" and therefore receiving the lowest price.

To get started, you should contact ICS with as much detail as possible about your business and its trading activities.

For further information, contact:

Mr. Kishore K. Sakhrani, Director
ICS Trust (Asia) Limited
8th Floor, Henley Building
Five Queen's Road, Central
Hong Kong
Telephone: +852 2854 4544
Fax: +852 2543 5555

You will be well-advised and well-serviced in the hands of this fine company.

Sources of Help for Offshore Investing

Britannia Corporate Management Limited

Another business specializing in the formation of offshore corporations and trusts is Britannia Corporate Management Limited, located in the Cayman Islands. Its president, Gary F. Oakley, is a Canadian with over 18 years of Cayman Islands residency. Britannia is licensed to manage investment holding and trading companies, real estate holding companies, patent holding companies, and insurance holding companies. It is licensed to incorporate and manage corporations registered in the Cayman Islands. As such, the firm can service as the registered office of a corporation, provide its secretary, officers and directors, or undertake any day-to-day functions that may be required. More information can be obtained by writing the following:

Britannia Corporate Management Limited
Attn: New Clients Information
P. O. Box 1968
Whitewall Estates, Grand Cayman
Cayman Islands

Britannia can be reached by fax at +1 345 949 0716, marking your fax "Attention New Clients Information.

Skye Fiduciary Services Limited

Skye Fiduciary Services Limited are among the foremost experts in offshore planning. Under the direction of its chairman Charles Cain, formerly managing director of the second merchant bank to open in the Isle of Man, Skye Fiduciary is the most experienced offshore corporate and trust management business in the jurisdiction. Although Skye offers a full range of company and trust management services, their expertise in designing novel company structures to meet the needs of foreign clients is unique.

For further information, write the following:

Skye Fiduciary Services Limited
Attn: New Clients Department
2 Water Street
Ramsey, Isle of Man 1M8 1JP
United Kingdom

Their telephone number is +44 1624 816117. Fax service is available at +44 1624 816645; marking your fax "Attention: New Clients Information".

JML Swiss Investment Counsellors

One of the leaders in Swiss financial management is JML Swiss Investment Counsellors, a firm which offers a unique style of financial management. Clients can customize and control their own portfolios and still receive comprehensive management advice from some of the world's best experts on financial matters.

Recognizing that investors have differing goals, time frames, and tolerance for risk, JML's managers work with their individual clients to help them target their unique objectives. This naturally requires continued surveillance and analysis of worldwide economic trends, political events, financial markets, currencies, and other factors which could make some investments particularly attractive and others most unfavorable. Few individuals have the time or expertise to undertake this kind of evaluation themselves.

Further information about JML can be obtained by writing the following:

JML Jurg M. Lattmann AG
Swiss Investment Counsellors
Germaniastrasse 55, Dept. 212
CH-8033 Zurich, Switzerland

Their telephone number is (41) 1 368-8233 and their fax number is (41) 1 368-8299, marking your fax "Attention Department 212".

Weber Hartmann Vrijhof & Partners

While there are many excellent Swiss investment financial managers, another one of particular note is the management firm of Weber Hartmann Vrijhof & Partners. Offering management services for the portfolios of both individuals and companies, the firm excels at providing personal attention to its clients. Weber Hartmann Vrijhof & Partners was established in 1992 by Hans Weber, Robert Vrijhof, and Adrian Hartmann. The three men have substantial experience in finance and investment. Weber managed Foreign

Commerce Bank (FOCOBANK) in Switzerland for nearly 30 years as its president and CEO, Vrijhof was a former vice-president and head of FOCOBANK'S portfolio management group, and Hartmann was head of FOCOBANK'S North American subsidiary in Vancouver. Weber Hartmann Vrijhof & Partners offers specialized investment services designed to meet the individual needs of their clients.

The minimum opening portfolio to be managed by this firm is $250,000 or equivalent. The management team here normally recommends that a portion of the portfolio be invested in hard currencies other than the U.S. dollar including the Swiss franc, French franc, German mark, and Dutch guilder. Respected for their conservative approach to portfolio management, the partners assist clients with opening a custodial account at one of the major private Swiss banks, so that all client securities are held by the bank, not the investment manager.

A large percentage of their clients are based in the United States. One of their main goals has always been to get a certain portion of their clients' wealth out of the U.S. dollar and into European hard currencies such as Swiss francs, Deutschmarks, and Dutch guilders, and then build a portfolio with a mix of bonds and shares.

For more information, you can write to the following:

Weber Hartmann Vrijhof & Partners Ltd.
Attn: New Clients Department
Zurichshstrasse 110B
CH-8134 Adilswil, Switzerland

Their telephone number is (41-1) 709-11-15 and their fax number (41-1) 709-11-13, marking your fax "Attention New Clients Department".

Dunn & Hargitt International Group

Recently, many international investors have become dissatisfied with the small annual return on Euro-dollar deposits.

This is why private and institutional investors throughout the world are looking at other areas where returns can be in the area of 20-25% a year, to help offset the high annual rates of inflation on luxury goods.

The Dunn & Hargitt International Group, founded in 1961, has specialized in doing research for developing Portfolio Management Programs that have the potential of providing investors with a high return on their capital by investing in a diversified portfolio trading in the commodity, currency, precious metals, and financial futures markets in the United States and throughout the world.

The Dunn & Hargitt group offers investors the possibilitiy of participating in several of the different pools that are managed by them by investing through the investment programs that are offered by their affiliate, Winchester Life in Gibraltar, but which are actually managed by The Dunn & Hargitt International Group.

At the time of publication they are offering three possible investment alternatives, including The Winchester Life Umbrella Account (which allows 100% of a client's money to be invested in a diversified futures portfolio), The Winchester Life 100% Guaranteed Investment Account (in which Lloyds Bank acts as custodian trustee and US Government Zero Coupon Treasury Bonds are set aside to guarantee the client's capital), and The Winchester Life 150% Guaranteed Investment Account (which is a similar program, but guaranteeing that the client will receive at least 150% of the value deposited with a maturity date at least ten years in the future).

The average net return for the 150% Guaranteed Investment Account over the last six years would have been 22% a year. The average net return on the 100% Guaranteed Investment Account over the last six years would have been 27% a year. The average annual net return for The Winchester Life Umbrella Account over the last twelve years would have been 35% a year.

The minimum accounts accepted are $20,000 for The Winchester Life Umbrella Account, $20,000 for The Winchester Life 100% Guaranteed Account, and $50,000 for The Winchester Life 150% Guaranteed Account.

Although commodities are a speculative form of investment, investors everywhere are diversifying part of their portfolios to take part in the considerable potential profit opportunities that are available in the commodity, currency, precious metals and financial futures markets. The programs devised by the Dunn & Hargitt International Group will make profits if significant trends develop in either direction; i.e. up or down. This does not mean that short term results are always profitable, however the Dunn & Hargitt proven trading systems can provide above average returns over the longer term. Their objective is to make a profit for their clients of between 20% and 40% per annum and their computer trading systems are geared to this level of performance.

For more information, contact:

The Dunn & Hargitt International Group
c/o Dunn & Hargitt Research S.A.
Department S-697
P.O. Box 3186
Road Town, Tortola
British Virgin Islands

The structure of the Dunn & Hargitt Group has been established so that no taxes are withheld from the client's investment on the international commodity, currency, precious metals and financial futures markets. Because of this they can only manage money for investors who are neither citizens nor residents of the United States.

The Dunn & Hargitt International Group offers complete confidentiality to all of its clients, and will not reveal any information on a client or on its accounts to any third parties.

About the Author

This special afterword was prepared by Adam Starchild who over the past 25 years has been the author of over two dozen books, and hundreds of magazine articles, primarily on business and finance. His articles have appeared in a wide range of publications around the world — including *Business Credit, Euromoney, Finance, The Financial Planner, International Living, Offshore Financial Review, Reason, Tax Planning International, The Bull & Bear, Trust & Estates*, and many more.

Now semi-retired, he was the president of an international consulting group specializing in banking, finance and the development of new businesses, and director of a trust company.

Although this formidable testimony to expertise in his field, plus his current preoccupation with other books-in-progress, would not seem to leave time for a well-rounded existence, Starchild has won two Presidential Sports Awards and written several cookbooks, and is currently involved in a number of personal charitable projects.

His personal website is at http://www.adamstarchild.com

www.ingramcontent.com/pod-product-compliance
Lightning Source LLC
Chambersburg PA
CBHW071940220326
41599CB00033BA/6592